CELTIC
WARRINGTON
& OTHER
MYSTERIES

COVER PHOTO: SEPTEMBER SUNRISE OVER RIXTON.

CELTIC WARRINGTON

& OTHER MYSTERIES

VOLUME ONE

WARRINGTON NORTH TO EAST

MARK OLLY

Published by

CHURNET VALLEY BOOKS

43 Bath Street
Leek
Staffordshire
01538 399033

All Photographs by Mark Olly unless otherwise stated. Maps & illustrations drawn or adapted from the Book of Deer, Book of Kells, Book of Durrow and Victorian copper plate engravings by Mark Olly, except the Swan Pub, Winwick, by Frank Brice

ISBN 1 897949 43 X

DEDICATED TO MY CHILDREN
LUKE MEL, SAMUEL RUEBEN, MARK OBED, ADAM JOSHUA
& CASSANDRA ROWAN

FOR THEIR CHILDREN

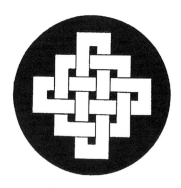

A BIG THANK YOU TO:

Many people have helped greatly in the production of this book, most especially: Mum & Dad, Heather
Olly, Doug & Hilary Pickford, Miles Fordham, Mike Nevell at The University of Manchester
Archeological Unit, Greater Manchester Archaeological Unit and Archive, Jenny Woodcock & Susi White
at the former Liverpool University Archaeological Unit, Martin Patch at The Manchester Museum (Celtic
Heads Study), Jill Collens at County Sites & Ancient Monuments Cheshire, Alan Leigh (Curator) & all
his staff at Warrington Museum & Library Service, Revd. Bob Lewis & Frank Brice at Winwick Church,
Caroline Davis & Andy Vosper at U.K. Waste Management Ltd., Rose & Carol Lythgoe at Warburton
Park, all the staff at SuperSnaps on Bridge Street, Warrington (Sue, Audrey & Linda), Bill Griffiths &
family, Alyn Adam, Andrew Sim, Wayne Percival, Len, Butler & family, Everyone at 'The Door Histories,
Mysteries & Discoveries Group', Warrington, Bruce Richardson & everyone at Churnet Valley Books in Leek.

FOREWORD

The series of books of which this is the first is intended as a practical guide to actual sites which can be visited in the region at this time, as well as giving basic background information required to view these sites from a more informed perspective. With this in mind, this book is arranged in the order best suited to a circular clockwise car journey through the area covered.

Technical information will only be included if it is important to the story in hand and all archaeological information has been summarised to make it readily understandable to ordinary folk! I do not intend this series of books to be factually exhaustive. The majority of people simply want to experience the existence of local history on a 'first hand' basis, without losing the joy of discovery.

The books are primarily a guide, secondarily a collection of useful or mysterious information otherwise hard to find and thirdly the start of a greater system of mysteries which surround the town and go back into very ancient history. In the final book of this series I hope to look at the full mystery of the town that is Warrington, a mystery which still lies veiled at this time, appearing only briefly to baffle and confound the unwary time-traveller.

My apologies if you know something I have left out or if I have made mistakes along the way. This kind of history is a life-long journey in which we are constantly moving and learning. I only hope to share my knowledge of the town in which I was born, and inspire others to look beyond the concrete and glass, back into the days of wood and stone where ancient 'Wise Ones' and 'God-Fearers' still sit, waiting to teach us how to live lightly and leave the earth prepared for our children - from whom it is only borrowed.

Mark Olly April 1998

CONTENTS

THE ROADS OF ENGLAND.

THE ROADS OF "MERRIE ENGLAND"
    ARE LIKE A MOTLEY THRONG -
FOR SOME ARE RATHER SHORT ROADS,
    AND OTHERS RATHER LONG -
THEN SOME ARE SOFT AND SANDY
    WANDERING TO AND FRO
AS IF THEY FEEL UNCERTAIN
    OF JUST THE WAY TO GO.
SOME ROADS ARE BLACK AND SHINY
    AND NEW AS NEW CAN BE;
BUT OTHER ROADS ARE OLD ROADS
    O'ERHUNG WITH MYSTERY,
ALL PEOPLED WITH THE SHADES
    OF BRITAIN'S ANCIENT HISTORY.
THE ROADS OF "MERRIE ENGLAND"
    ARE NEVER TWICE THE SAME,
AND EVERY TIME YOU FOLLOW THEM
    YOU THANK THE LORD YOU CAME.

L.B.D.

"WARRINGTON WALKS" - WARRINGTON ENTERPRISE (NEWSPAPER) JULY 1927.

INTRODUCTION

It would be of great help to the reader to buy the four relevant Ordnance Survey maps covering Warrington in the 'Pathfinder' series, these being numbers 722, 723, 739, 740 and the Geographer's A-Z street plan of Warrington. All location maps shown in this book have been 'regressed' in an attempt to remove modern developments and give a flavour of the areas in Celtic times; only modern route-roads are shown as single lines.

Fortunately a great body of work already exists to assist our Celtic travels but the first step is to define exactly what we mean by the Celtic period. For the purposes of this study the Celtic period can be taken as emerging from the mists of the Late Neolithic Period or New Stone Age around 2500 years BC and developing into distinct Celtic cultures about 1000 BC through the Bronze & Iron ages, fading out at some point after 900 AD with the establishment of early Christianity in Britain and the invasion of the Saxons, Danes, Norse and finally the Normans in 1066 AD.

Some authorities maintain that the Celtic period continued right up to 1300 AD and beyond but a better term for this period would be 'Early Medieval' (although 'Celts' may still survive in Ireland, Scotland and Wales in some form even to this day - more of this later). With this in mind, the reader should excuse the odd drift into medieval times should the subject matter dictate.

It already goes without saying that the very nature of mystery which surrounds the Celts begins with obscure prehistoric European origins and ends with their gradual fading from the pages of history. They rose with the Druids who may have built Stonehenge and blended, chameleon-like, into the framework of the early Christian church as it evangelised Britain long after the Romans had departed for home.

The second step in the voyage of discovery is to choose a method of travel appropriate to the trip in hand. In this case I have chosen to divide Warrington into a 'clock' with 12.00 set at North, 3.00 at East, 6.00 at South and 9.00 at West with Bridge Street and the 'River Of Life' sculpture in Warrington town centre as the central point. So great is the quantity of information that each quarter will be dealt with in a separate book of similar length, culminating in the 'Grand De-Coda', a fifth and final volume written to summarise the whole. However, it is important that the reader should buy all the volumes irrespective of area in order to fully grasp the Celtic town of Warrington. All areas are directly related.

This present volume is book one of the series and deals with sites in a clockwise direction starting at Winwick (12.00 o'clock) and ending at Warburton (3.00 o'clock) with all areas in that quarter included and mostly found on Ordnance Survey Pathfinder 723 and the top of 740.

The third and final requirement to any voyage of mystery is a certain aptitude for the unseen, a sort of 'sixth sense' awareness of the stars, nature, magic, belief, etc. To this end I have included a small element of the more esoteric such as ley lines, geomantic details, underground water sources, star alignments and sacred sites as well as the more recognised sciences of archaeology, cartography, geology and paleantology.

This book began with a comment passed by an employee of the local museum three years ago in response to the question, "What was Warrington like before the Romans?" His answer was the same as many Warringtonians would have given: "There was no Warrington before the Romans." Not so, my friend!

BEYOND THE ANCIENT MISTS OF TIME

Before our area of the British Isles became an established centre for settlement, the Ice Age had left the district covered with a thick layer of boulder clay which was most apparent during the building of the Manchester Ship Canal when a layer between six and sixteen feet thick (1.9m-5.2m) had to be removed before the solid underlying rock could be found. As these glacial ice sheets retreated, the Mersey valley gradually became a fertile, wooded enclave with animals useful to Stone Age hunters.

Early this century a magnificent pair of deer antlers were found during excavations of a sand pit at Bob's Bridge, between Warrington and Runcorn (site now lost) and two red deer antler picks were found as the Manchester Ship Canal cut its way out of Warrington to the east, past the mosslands, one in 1894 and one in 1897. More recently red deer remains were found in October 1995 by North West Water on their Gatewarth

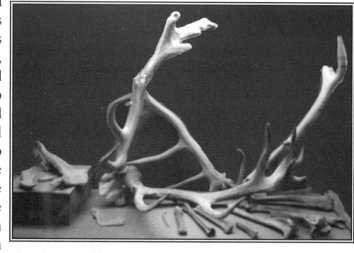

Sewerage Works in Sankey Bridges. These included two complete pairs of antlers over 3 feet (1m) long and 3 ins (7cm) thick accompanied by a small antler, the complete lower jawbone and a fragment of a lower jaw from two horses and at least ten other assorted

animal bones all dated to 1000 BC. Another red deer antler was recently unearthed close to Warrington town centre during the construction of the East-West bypass in 1996.

So far, I have not found any records of Palaeolithic burials in the region, which would lead to the conclusion that the plains of Lancashire and Cheshire were used mainly for hunting rather than settlement, although ancient bones would not preserve well in this area. Stray finds of implements plotted on a map seem to support this view and form a link, like milestones along a highway, connecting known settlements of the east with those in the west. Ancient established tracks can be traced along the southern banks of the Mersey and Irwell to the Calder and on into Yorkshire. At Warrington there are routes on both sides of the Mersey indicating a very early crossing point or 'ford' here well before the Romans. By Neolithic times some animals had been domesticated by early settlers in Warrington, such as the dog and the uru or oxen (very much like a large water buffalo). The perfect skull of an uru was found at Walton Lock when the Ship Canal was being cut, along with two of the famous dug-out canoes and a settlement structure (more of this in book three). There also exists one report from this period of the discovery of a bear skull during canal cutting operations. Warrington Museum presently have three very early human skulls on display found locally. There are two complete heads without jaws and one crown section only, which have been found in the River Mersey at various times and may have belonged to the earliest settlers of Warrington, dating back to beyond the early Iron Age.

The major Neolithic route North from the Mersey crossing sets the starting line for our first journey into Celtic Warrington. This will be our twelve o'clock from which the hands of time swing clockwise from the Druid's temple at Winwick, through Croft, Culcheth and Glazebury. Then on through Chat Moss, Rixton with Glazebrook and finishing with the Knights Templar monastery at Warburton and the modern sites of Birchwood, built in the true 'Celtic spirit'. The car journey begins at Winwick church....

CONSTRUCTION BARGE MOORED ON THE 'NEW CUT' OF THE
MANCHESTER SHIP CANAL.

THE AREAS OF

WINWICK

CROFT

CULCHETH

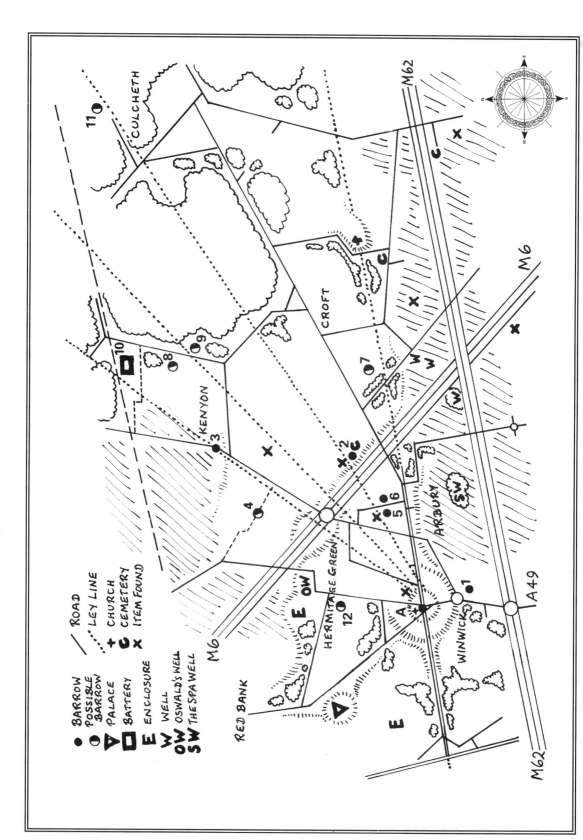

WINWICK

BIRTH OF A CELTIC CITY

In his book *Winwick: Its History And Antiquities* published in 1879, William Beamont states that the learned historian Usher made Winwick one of twenty cities collected by the 6th century Celtic historian Gildas out of the 5th century Irish Celtic writings of a British chronicler monk known as 'Nennius'. Its name at that time was 'CAER GWENTQUIC' (hence WENTWICK = WINWICK) around 400 AD.

Another story is recorded in the 1859 publication *Choice Notes From 'Notes And Queries Magazine' - Folk Lore* that a pig was seen moving stones from the original site of Winwick church to its present site, crying "We-ee-wick, We-ee-wick!" as it ran; hence WEEWICK = WINWICK (but more of this pig later).

An equally fascinating theory makes the name Saxon in origin from 'WIN' and 'WICK' meaning 'the place of fight or victory'. This could be possible considering the Saxons were in Winwick at the time of the death of King Oswald of Northumbria in battle against the King of Mercia in August 642 AD.

Our story, however, begins over 2000 years before this date, back in the Neolithic or Late Stone Age period where the Celts themselves also began.

FROM STONE TO METAL

The midsummer sunrise peered cautiously over the flat top of a Neolithic barrow and marker stone, casting a long shadow towards the platform of a wide stone ring a mile to the west. A procession of cloaked figures turned right off the Roman Highway and began a slow climb along the westerly approach avenue to the sacred man-made hill. Down a similar easterly avenue came villagers from the surrounding settlements to witness the solstice ceremony marking the turning point of the year. Druids also came from the eastern peat-lands and forests.

The villagers surrounded the outer stones as the Druid priests entered, honouring the graves of ancient giant chieftains before the midsummer solstice light filled the ancient temple. This was not Stonehenge but Winwick.

There are six basic categories of burial mound given in Archaeology:
- Isolated Long Barrows (Broad Barrows),
- Domed upward Bowl and Bell Barrows (Cone Barrows),
- Druid Barrows with stone or mound surrounds and/or ditches,
- Flat or inverted Disc Barrows (Pond Barrows),
- Stone Barrows (Cairns, Carnedd) which generally have no earth or stone covering,
- Crop or soil rings - burial features that show up on aerial photographs and cannot, therefore, be placed in any of the other categories.

One of these 'cropmarks' representing the site of a former round barrow was located in a cereal crop by Rob Philpott in 1991 while flying over Winwick village. This is approximately marked **1** on the map showing Prehistoric and Bronze Age finds in the Winwick area.

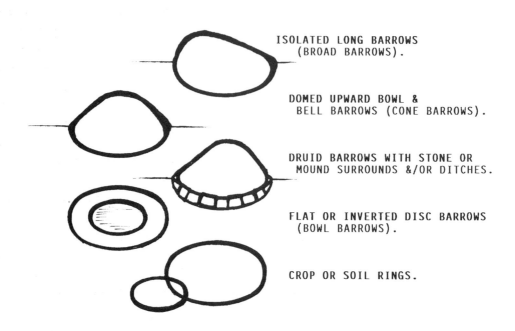

ISOLATED LONG BARROWS
(BROAD BARROWS).

DOMED UPWARD BOWL &
BELL BARROWS (CONE BARROWS).

DRUID BARROWS WITH STONE OR
MOUND SURROUNDS &/OR DITCHES.

FLAT OR INVERTED DISC BARROWS
(BOWL BARROWS).

CROP OR SOIL RINGS.

The first barrow mentioned in the ceremony story appears on the distant crest of a ridge at **2** on the map. This barrow has yielded a surprising variety of finds dealt with in detail later under the 'Sacred Sites' sections on Croft where the barrow is situated. Another barrow appears on the 1953 O.S. map at **3** next to Kenyon Hall Farm and may mark a major solar standstill when viewed from Winwick church mound in ancient times (which is marked as **A**). A bronze awl (needle) and nine pottery urn fragments were ploughed up from this mound in 1826. Three Bronze Age urn burials and the tongue of a bronze brooch were also recovered in 1903 just before the A579 to Lowton destroyed the mound. The overall hill site does still remain and may have contained more than one barrow as three O.S. references are given for finds in the Cheshire Sites & Monuments Record.

The 1953 O.S. map also reveals a short road off the A579 called 'Barrow Lane' which may have been in the proximity of another barrow in ancient times. This road has now become disused because of the M6 motorway and the cottages it served have been demolished. It is approximately marked as **4** and barrows **2-4** mark solar alignments possibly dating as far back as 2000+ BC.

Possibly the oldest find recovered from the Winwick area was discovered by a pupil of Golborne Secondary School in the early 1960s. Alan Glover found a reddish-orange prehistoric flint dagger in a potato field just north-east of Oven Back Farm on the A579 Winwick Road, and, when the school gave it to Liverpool Museum in 1965, it proved to be of very fine workmanship and an extremely rare type for Western Britain.

Another 1000 years closer to our time, at **5** and **6** stood a double bell barrow dating to the Middle or Late Bronze Age, which was romantically called "Robin Hood's Butts" up to the end of the nineteenth century. The mound at **5** was excavated in 1852 when workmen under the direction of a Dr.Kendrick uncovered many bone and pottery fragments. Again in 1859 the mound was "carefully explored by a party of gentlemen from Warrington and the neighbourhood" with similar results. The majority remains unexcavated (although heavily farmed) and no incidental finds are recorded - possibly due to the mound being invaded by a mains sewer. D.Longley in his book *Prehistoric Sites In Cheshire* says that it was surmounted by "an old tower" up to the 1960s or 1970s.

In 1844 an urn was found in the mound at **6**, and between 1859 and 1864 (principally in February of 1860,) the mound was levelled to fill up a large ditch nearby and produced three collections of urn fragments (aprox: 7, 11 and 15 pieces), one complete urn containing bones, a stone hammer head and a bronze dart (or short dagger blade). The mound was finally removed completely for farming purposes in 1879. The Liverpool University rescue dig of 1980 found only poor features remaining and the base of a small Bronze Age bowl.

Also in the collection of Warrington Museum are two bronze 'palstave' type axe heads (also known as 'celts') simply shown as being "found at Winwick". One was found with a large bronze ring (possibly used to stop the shaft splitting), and the other socketed axe has an unusual chevron decoration. All are reported as being found between 1858 and 1860. In the book 'The Archaeology Of Warrington's Past' produced by a team of researchers for the former Warrington New Town, the site at which these bronze items were found in Hermitage Green is identified as a tumulus although no burials are recorded as being found. This is marked as **12** on the map.

In his report of the exploration of "Robin Hood's Butts", Dr. Kendrick states that "A third barrow of an equal size, formerly existed about a quarter of a mile to the east." No trace of this barrow now remains however it is marked **7** on the map at the most likely approximate location given the information available. It is unlikely that this barrow was a confusion with the one at **2**, Southworth Hall, Croft, as this barrow was fairly well known at the time.

Two other, as yet unidentified, burial mounds may have existed in the area of Barrow's Farm and Lowe's Farm further out at **8** and **9**, both farms being named after ancient burial sites, but no evidence of any other mounds in Winwick has been found by archaelogical surveys so far.

A curious feature appears on early O.S. maps as 'Beard's Battery' at **10**. This feature can be reached down the best preserved example of a Victorian cobbled lane now existing in Warrington (Main Lane) and looks like a large square of earth, possibly raised during the English Civil War as a cannon battery (which is the first time the term 'battery' was employed for a gun emplacement). Local tradition says that the structure was erected at this time in order to shell Winwick church, or it was used for rifle practice during the Second World War. This does not rule out the possibility that the original structure could be much older as no Civil War battle requiring cannon is recorded as taking place in the Kenyon area.

Back to the large mound at Winwick Church (**A**). I will quote directly from William Beamont's 1879 book:

> *"In the account of Winwick printed by Mr. Calvert (?) he mentions as existing there a tradition that the church occupied the site of a Druidical altar and*

also of a Pagan temple. The hill on which the church stands and which may have been raised above its original height by artificial means, seems likely enough to have recommended it as the place of sepulture in a dark age, and that it had been so used we have evidence in the discovery made in 1828, when digging under the chancel they found at the depth of eight or ten feet below the floor, and buried under a heap of sandstone blocks, varying from one to two feet in size, three human skeletons of a gigantic stature. The skeletons seem to have been laid one upon another, but no remains of coffins were discovered with them."

Here we have the burial mound of the "Winwick Giants" probably dating back beyond the Bronze Age to the late Stone Age or Middle Neolithic Period 2750 to 2250 BC (as the bodies would have been cremated in the Bronze Age) and answering the description of a 'Druids Barrow' or "Druids Altar" (several of these also existed at Grappenhall). One local legend, still current in the 1950s, gave the heights for the Winwick skeletons as 7ft 2ins, 7ft 4ins and 7ft 8ins, all male.

There is no doubt, from the evidence of the alignments, that Winwick was a special site of importance and worship. Although I can presently find no trace of any standing stones remaining in the vicinity of the church, they will almost certainly have been there as markers, in order for the positions of the burial mounds to be so accurately aligned to the stars, sun and moon in relation to this mound.

A dig undertaken by Professor Stuart Piggott of Edinburgh University on a similar but undeveloped site at Cairnpapple Hill, West Lothian in 1947-48 revealed an almost exact sequence of finds and events to those

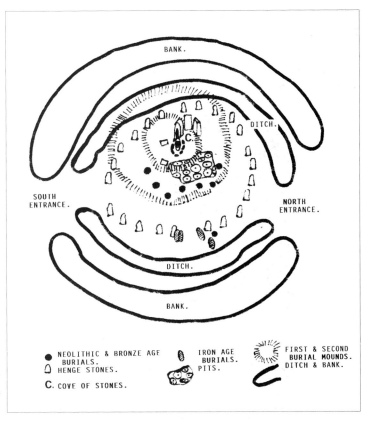

possible from the evidence at Winwick and the plan of this site is reproduced here. (Another significant clue to the existence of standing stones was unearthed at the barrow **2** covered later under the Croft area). Furthermore, if a comparison between a simple outline map of Avebury, Wiltshire, and Winwick is done (SEE ILLUSTRATIONS) the architectural similarities become instantly apparent.

The same alignments of mounds and roads and the same archaeological finds generally appear at all three sites in southern, middle and northern Britain. With regard to Avebury, Hollins Lane and Myddleton Lane correspond to the West and East entrances and the A49 Newton Road matches the North and South entrances with a Christian church structure constructed at the approximate centre in later times.

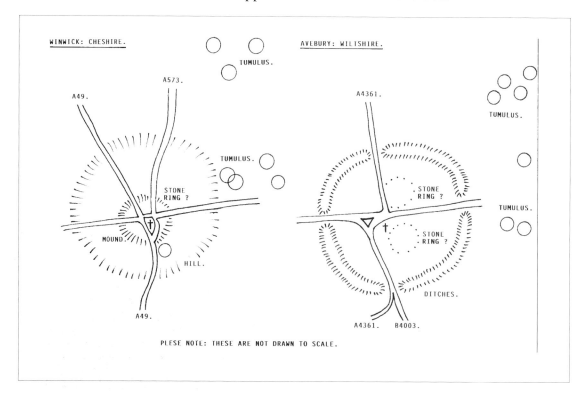

PLESE NOTE: THESE ARE NOT DRAWN TO SCALE.

AVENUES OF EVIDENCE AND EVIDENCE OF AVENUES

The Eastern avenue coming into the original sacred site on Winwick church mound (**A**) may have ended at the junction of Myddleton Lane and Delph Lane somewhere in the grounds of Stone House Farm where all the farm buildings are made from red brick and not stone as you might expect from the name. This may indicate that the 'stone' was actually a monolith which ended the avenue and was incorporated into the farmstead which was then named 'Stone House' - or that a monolith existed in that immediate vicinity, possibly at the barrow **2** on the ridge opposite (SEE SECTION ON CROFT).

In summer 1997 a deep pit was dug in the centre of the road just in front of Stone House Farm in order to put in a man-hole cover. This revealed that the first three to four feet depth (1m) contained at least twelve major and many minor road surfaces, starting with several layers of tarmac followed by 6 inch cobblestone sets then several feet of earlier road layers, before the underlying uniform ground layer was reached. This supports the long term continuous use of this route back into very ancient times; the average road surface (eg Bridge St, Warrington's main high street) will only be a maximum of two feet (less than 70cm).

THE NORTH -SOUTH A49 'RIDGEWAY' IN THE 1880'S.

Winwick church presently displays a print of cattle being driven down this road before it was cobbled early in the 19th century.

From here the Eastern avenue continues in the form of an ancient ley line which passes behind medieval Myddleton Hall where a damaged bronze age axe with a shield decoration was found in 1895, on through the possible burial mound at **7** and the church at Croft. Then through the former moated site of Old Abbey Farm, the mound and Iron Age settlement at Little Woolden Hall and out across Great Woolden Moss towards Irlam, eventually lining up with the A628 to Barnsley over the High Peak district Howden Moors.

THE EASTERN APPROACH ROAD IN THE EARLY NINETEENTH CENTURY.

Another line from Winwick church through barrow **2** at Croft eventually lines up with the A62 to Huddersfield which is the other major route over the Northern High Peak at Saddleworth Moor - both probable ancient ridgeway routes over the Pennines and beyond.

The Western avenue, going the other way out of Winwick, may run close to the present road or through both churches on the Winwick Hospital site, both of which sit on or next to the 'sacred line' down from the church mound. This line would have crossed the Roman highway in the fields beyond Winwick Hall Farm close to Sankey Brook, making Winwick a national port of call on the journey North or South on the Chester-Carlisle Roman road which ended at Hadrian's Wall.

The remains of the Roman road runs North through Wargrave, Newton Le Willows and beyond Ashton In Makerfield (which is probably the remnant of the 'Maserfelth' region where King Oswald died in battle). Greater Manchester Archaeological Unit excavated the line of the road at Alder Root Farm in 1992 and found the road intact but badly damaged by centuries of farming.

Further significance can be attached to the fact that the Romans chose not to drive this Northward highway through Winwick but rather to divert to the West and avoid the ancient mound by a safe distance. This would indicate great reverence for the site continuing through the Roman occupation of Britain and may also account for the legend of a "Pagan Temple" existing on the Winwick Mound, 'Pagan' often being equated with 'Roman' in days gone by. This is dealt with in the section on 'The Winwick Pig'.

From here the Western avenue develops into a ley line which links the two churches on the old hospital site with the Old Moat House at Burtonwood, Marshalls Cross (site of a Celtic cross and settlement) and Prescot hill, eventually passing through the centre of Liverpool, Birkenhead and the large Celtic/Viking port of Meols at Hoylake, finishing on the "Druids Isle" of Anglesey.

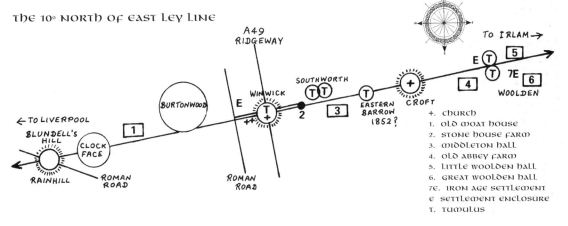

THE 10° NORTH OF EAST LEY LINE

+. church
1. OLD MOAT HOUSE
2. STONE HOUSE FARM
3. MIDDLETON HALL
4. OLD ABBEY FARM
5. LITTLE WOOLDEN HALL
6. GREAT WOOLDEN HALL
7E. IRON AGE SETTLEMENT
E SETTLEMENT ENCLOSURE
T. TUMULUS

CELTIC STRUCTURES IN WINWICK

Back again to the main Church mound at **A**. Following the development of the mound, stones and avenues during the late Stone Age came the giants' burial and the development of the sacred site during the Bronze Age. The next few steps in time indicate a more original development sequence than has previously been thought.

In order to protect the sacred site from the invading Romans who first came to the area between 43 and 50 AD, and to form a border defence for the northern kingdom of Northumbria, the mound and nearby settlement would probably have been fortified with a wooden motte and bailey structure, a pattern still apparent in the post-Victorian village plan. A ditch may have been dug at the base of the mound and an area on top improved to form a fenced stockade with gates containing the Stone Age

burial. Next to this stood an area of worship and, nearby, the home of the Celtic lord. Standing stones would have been removed completely or possibly incorporated into buildings and defences during these phases of settlement construction.

This new and detailed hypothesis is not without its support. Lt.Col.Henry Fishwick (FSA) in his book *A History Of Lancashire* published in the 'Popular County Histories' series of 1894 noted that, "Winwick, near Warrington, has also its traditional Saxon castle." Sadly he neglected to say where this castle was said to be! William Beamont also asserts that "Winwick was undoubtedly an early Lancashire parish, and the site first of a British and then of an ancient Saxon village", with *The History of Lancaster* by Edward Baines adding that "Winwick is supposed from its name to have been the seat of one of the twelve Saxon chiefs who formed their establishments in south Lancashire before the institution of parishes" (Bede).

This would have marked the start of the city of CAER GWENTQUICK mentioned by the Celtic historian Gildas who is thought to have written his accounts of Celtic life some time in the 6th century (500-600 AD) from Irish writings a decade older (400-500 AD).

Also included in this early development is the legend that a pig was involved in the building of the first stone sacred structure, indicating it may date back to the late Roman period. The ancient Pig or Boar was the ensign of the Twentieth Legion who crossed the Mersey between 71 and 74 AD. This legion would be a familiar visitor to Winwick as it garrisoned Hadrian's Wall during and after the wall's construction which began in 122 AD. Local folklore goes further to say that a detachment of soldiers was actually stationed at Winwick (Arbury) and had a Pig as its mascot.

Maybe this Roman 'pig' legion did indeed help to plant the foundations of the first church - their own Pagan temple structure - some time before 200 AD. The Celtic style column bases of the North church aisle may show two Roman column designs carved on the flat surfaces between each Celtic corner head. Three settlement enclosures have been detected in the Winwick area using aerial photography and a trial dig on one of these in 1994 produced Roman pottery from 100-200 AD.

Eventually the Romans made peace with the resident Celts at Warrington (as shown by discoveries at Wilderspool Roman Fort) and did not withdraw a military presence from Britain until about 410 AD.

B.Griffiths

WINWICK CHURCH AROUND 1900.

B.Griffiths

PRIMROSE HILL, WINWICK IN 1900, BUT WHERE WAS IT?

ARTHURIAN CONNECTIONS

Through the research of many noted scholars it is supposed that Arthur lived from about 475 AD to 515 AD, being born either in Wales, the Midlands or Cornwall and, his name means 'The Bear'. He eventually took the title 'Dux Brittanorum', Leader or Duke of Britain (not 'king' as popularly supposed), commanding the armies of various petty kings and chieftains ruling lands claimed after the Roman withdrawal in 410 AD. Had these private armies remained in disarray and fighting one another, Britain would have been wide open for invasion again from the continent. Arthur united them in the face of this very real possibility.

In the 'Dream Of Rhonabwy' from the Welsh *Mabinogion*, Arthur's original Celtic chivalric colours are believed to be given as "broom flower yellow" and "pine needle green". His emblem was said to be the Celtic wild pig or 'boar' which he had upon his shield in response to Merlin's prophecy of his coming as the "Boar of Cornwall". Interestingly this pig-shield was also said to have been the legendary arms of King Oswald (a later visitor to Winwick).

In his 1965 book *The Legacy Of Arthur's Chester*, Robert B.Stoker makes mention of occurences which have a bearing on the Arthurian 'Dark Age' period of Winwick. He surmises that King Arthur defeated the Northern Saxons twice at "the little River Douglas near Wiggin", once in 491 AD and again in 494 AD, two occasions that would have taken him through the Winwick area on his way to and from the former Roman city of Chester (then in Welsh-Celtic hands) via the Mersey ford at Warrington.

Arthur may even have stationed his forces for a time at Winwick, it being the nearest major fortified religious site from which to attack 'Wiggin' and the Saxons.

Merlin (Myrddin Wyllt) also has a connection with the sacred Celtic pig which was said to be his only companion while he lived wild in the woods. Could any of these be the first origin of the Winwick pig? Eventually Arthur passed away and the Saxons gained the final victory.

St.Oswald's is known to have been the mother church of a large and ancient parish of twelve or so Saxon townships forming the southern half of the Newton Hundred, which included the adjacent royal estate centre of Newton itself, and was ruled over by twelve minor kings in the post-Roman period. The large curvilinear churchyard shows signs of Celtic, Saxon and Viking influence and this has led archaeologists to identify it as a collegiate 'minster' site. Imagine the church being 'Winwick Minster'!

Between 605 and 607 AD even Chester had fallen to King Aethelfrith, the Saxon King of Northumbria, who would have marched through the Warrington district with his army claiming it for Northumbria, the county later ruled by the famous King Oswald.

VANISHING SWANS, CHURCHES AND PALACES

A TALE OF TWO SWANS

During the autumn of 1991 an interesting hard sandstone block about 20 inches high, 18 inches deep and 25 inches long (50cm x 45cm x 63cm) was removed from the front left side of The Swan public house, oposite the church, to allow the building of a dining extension. This block featured two outstanding carved swans facing each other with a simplified 'tree of life' design between them (SEE ILLUSTRATION). Sadly this carving has now disappeared but its significance lies in the Irish Nennius and Celtic tales of magic swans.

F. Brice

In Celtic legends the swans are a fair maid and her servant transformed, who the hero sinks by stoning but who rise from the waters as women again to show the breaking of enchantment by a blow and the concept of resurrection after death - as does the tree of life in Christian and Eastern thought. A swan's reflection also represented "this world and the next", both interpretations making this block a probable piece of the original Celtic chapel of Winwick. The mystery remains, however - where is it now?

THESE SWANS ARE A BIT OF A PHOTO MYSTERY. THEY ALL HAD THEIR USES BUT AS WHAT? THE LEFT ONE IS LEAD, THE FRONT PAIR ARE CAST IRON, THE BACK PAIR ARE SPELTER AND THE RIGHT ONE IS BRASS.

A TALE OF TWO CHURCHES

The giants' burial mound would have stood where the present church chancel stands. The Roman/Celtic house of worship later developed into the Northern side of the present church where a Celtic/Christian chapel was constructed in stone and the lord's manor house may be sited somewhere to the North under Church Walk or further on towards the site of the later Priory. By Oswald's day the manor house had moved even further North to a site of its own.

At this time the Celtic lord's manor and pre-Celtic churches lie buried below existing structures awaiting discovery. However, several items of interest lie inside the present church structure to support the theories so far proposed. The key for the church can presently be obtained from the Rectory a few hundred yards further up the A573 Golbourne Road, past the Post Office, on the left hand side of the road.

The church guide book attributes the five decorated column bases which make up the Gerrard Chapel supports in the North aisle to Norman times (1190-1250 AD), based on the identification of the carved heads bearing a 'hat' being that of a Norman bishop wearing a mitre. Although a church is recorded at Winwick in the Domesday Book of 1086 AD, the structure then long pre-dated the survey. The bishop theory also makes no allowance for the presence of a second set of heads on the bases with a 'curvy' hair style or 'hood' like a dutch hat and details of two Roman column bases in miniature on each flat face.

In reality the column bases more likely date back to the very first Celtic/Christian stone chapel to stand on the site, built some time after the death of King Oswald in 645 AD and probably replacing the earlier Roman and wooden Celtic sacred structures on the site about 700-800 AD. The head with the 'hat' is King Oswald wearing a Celtic war helmet and the other head with odd hair or 'hood' is that of St.Anthony, to whom the church is dedicated.

A 3rd century (200-300 AD) stone plaque has been found in Northumberland dedicated to the religious order of 'Genii Culcullati', the 'Hooded Ones', and depicts

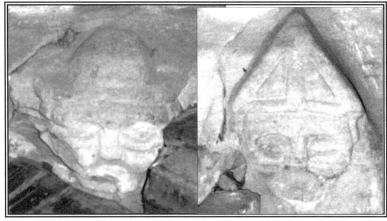

three of these mysterious holy men wearing hooded cloaks. Another even older image of a Gallic warrior has been found at Sainte-Anastasie in Gard, France, wearing a similar 'hood' to the St.Anthony face of Winwick. This figure has also been interpreted as a 'Gennius Culcullatus' and the hood as representing the head shrouded in the 'womb' or 'caul' of rebirth. It is not too far-fetched to suggest that the later Celtic stone masons visualised St.Anthony as a 'born-again Gennius Culcullatus', or Christian holy man.

Further support for the Oswald/Anthony hypothesis can be found in the comparison of a famous 5th century Celtic statue found on Boa Island, Lower Lough Erne, Co. Fermanagh, which bears an uncanny facial resemblance to the helmeted head and the other face with hair (SEE ILLUSTRATION).

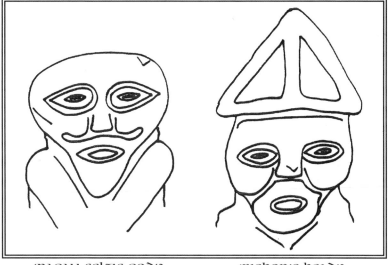

'PAGAN CELTIC GOD'?
CALDRAGH
NORTHERN IRELAND.

'BISHOP'S HEAD'?
WINWICK
WARRINGTON CHESHIRE

When the builders erected a set of arches on the South side of the centre aisle in 1836 they also continued the idea that the heads were Oswald and St.Anthony. They reproduced the heads from the column bases on the termination of each arch creating five identical pairs of Celtic-style heads alternately crowned as Oswald and uncrowned as St.Anthony. The miniature column details may represent earlier Roman columns present on the site at that time but now removed.

Another fragment of the later Celtic church structure could well be the ancient broken Anglo-Saxon stone font displayed on a modern pedestal in the Gerard Chapel, and once decorated with open flower heads. This was probably broken by Cromwell's men during the Civil War along with the huge Celtic Cross, the arms of which are presently to the right of the font on the window ledge of the Chapel. Dating from after the death of Oswald in 645 AD, this cross, dug up in the churchyard in 1873, would have stood outside the stone chapel (possibly on the burial mound) as a focus for preaching by the early monks, and could have stood as high as 30 feet or more when compared to the very similar famous cross of St.Martin on Iona. It was probably carved by the same masons associated with the missionaries brought from Iona by Oswald. A date of 700-800 AD has also been assigned to this cross arm.

It is an interesting thought that the rest of this ancient cross may still lie buried in the churchyard waiting to be discovered - if only we knew the exact location of the cross arm found in 1873! It is also said that this cross replaced an earlier, much simpler cross erected by Bishop Paulinus of York between 625 and 632 AD when he came north for the marriage of Princess Ethelburga of Kent to King Edwin of Northumbria, Oswald's Uncle.

Carved on one end of the cross is a figure (possibly a monk or priest) carrying water from Oswald's Well. On the other end two of Penda's soldiers have hung the defeated Oswald from a tree and are preparing to dismember his body which already appears to have no hands and stretched entrails. This leads into the important local Celtic legends surrounding the death of King Oswald which are detailed in the next chapter.

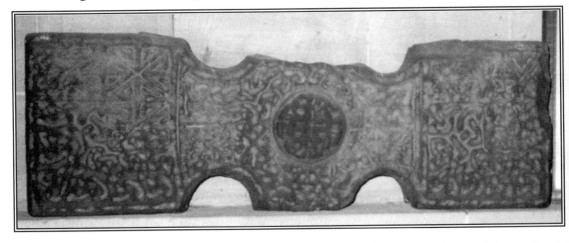

Some time early this century a Mr.Pearce produced his own obscure history book for Winwick church entitled *St.Oswald's Winwick* in which appeared the following:

"There is (what appears to be) a mermaid carved upon a stone on the west wall of the south isle. We suggest the builders of our church retained some fond memory of Mer Essy? - a Pre-Christian Nymph of Mersey?"

Having searched for this item in our present time, the only remaining traces detected are the arms, torso and battered face(?) of a figure carved on a stone of the outside wall which joins the aisle to the tower. Apparently the figure was far more distinct before the church was cleaned after the war and it may also be set into the wall upside-down! Is this the mysterious 'Mer Essy' or, like the swans, has she simply disappeared? If this figure is inverted, what building was it originally part of?

To cast a little doubt on the 'Mer Essy' legend, Lt.Col. Fishwick wrote in his 1894 book *A History Of Lancashire* that in pre-Christian times (if Christianity first came with the Romans) the river Mersey was actually called the "Estuary Belisama" by the geographer Ptolemy writing of three Lancashire estuaries in 140 AD. Therefore 'Belisama' was actually the only pre-Christian name for the Mersey conclusively recorded and to this day no one has been able to establish the English root or age of the name 'Mersey' which may simply mean 'boarder'.

It is noticeable that there is an absence of the Celtic 'Green Man' or 'foliate head' motif so common in ancient churches everywhere but not at Winwick. While early builders studiously avoided including the design, the Victorians who built the Chancel, Sanctuary and Altar between 1847 and 1849 included it as the spout from the Piscina basin (used for washing chalices) set into the wall on the right hand side of the Altar. Holy water falling to the sacred ground to drain does so now through the mouth of the Green Man - Celtic symbol of fertility. (This Green Man appears at the head of the chapter "Birchwood, Locking Stumps and Risley").

A TALE OF TWO PALACES

Beyond the church and main mound, two other legendary sites deserve a mention. During his brief reign of about 8 years from 634 to 642 AD, King Oswald is said to have had a 'summer palace' residence on the outskirts of Winwick at one of two locations to the west and north.

In his book *Winwick, Its History And Antiquities*, William Beamont states that "An ancient tradition is current that Bradley (Old) Hall, about three miles from Winwick, an old moated mansion with an ancient massive and ponderous stone gateway, was one of the residences of Oswald." The site certainly dates back before King Richard III stayed there in the late 15th century, possibly back to the Norman invasion of Cheshire in 1070 AD, but evidence of any older habitation is lacking despite the impressive water-filled moat and medieval gateway. The moat was recently dredged and produced only Victorian pottery and the oldest item so far found by the owner in the fields surrounding has been a Cromwellian cannon ball.

Other local traditions make the mound north of the church at Red Bank (also the site of the Civil War battle of 1648 AD) the site of the summer palace. This would place it buried somewhere below, or next to, Cop Holt Farm by the A49 Newton Road (the Celtic

'ridgeway') and perhaps add to the later Civil War story - it being still a defendable and fortified mound from past centuries at that time. Enquiries of the present owners reveal no finds of any kind to date but the mound has been extensively farmed and various ancient stones do litter the farm yard and drive. This site is probably the more likely location for Oswald's palace but any remains may have been completely destroyed and the private mound is not open to public access.

Two other enclosures have been identified by aerial photography in this area; a single-ditched version was excavated without results in 1987 behind Lower Alder Root Farm and a double-ditched site was found in 1966 behind Hermitage Farm near St.

Oswald's Well. Either of these may prove to have connections with Oswald and the local Celts.

This photo shows the inside of the gate house front arch and one of the roof buttress supports on the left.

KING OSWALD AND THE SACRED WELLS

No complete narrative of the death of King Oswald has been attempted as far as I am able to find, although the various parts have been recorded in many publications over the years. Therefore, here is an attempt to summarise these accounts.

Born in 605 AD Prince of Northumbria, Oswald became King between 633 and 634 AD, firstly, following his victory over the Welsh King Cadwallon near Hexham where he gained back the Kingdom of his father Ethelfrith, and secondly following the death of his uncle King Edwin during a battle in 638 AD.

A Christian himself, he was eager to bring Christianity to his subjects and brought over Irish priests and holy men from Icolmkill (now known as the Isle of Iona) where he was taught as a youth. These holy men probably included St.Wilfred, St.Aidan (later Bishop of Lindisfarne) and St.Elfin (to whom is dedicated the Parish Church of Warrington first built at this time). This is possibly one key to understanding the very early ties Warrington has with Ireland which still exist to this day.

During his brief reign Oswald married Princess Cyneburga, daughter of Cynegils, the first Christian King of Wessex, and had some overlordship in most of the other Celtic Kingdoms in Britain.

Hearing of Oswald's religious endeavours and growing fame, the Pagan King Penda of Merci. (who assumed the title 'king' as early as 626 AD and seems to have been a trouble to everybod. from then on) entered with a surprise invasion force and engaged Oswald at Maserfelth (o. Maserfeld) on August 5th 642 AD. Penda was about 66, Oswald only 37. No one knows wher. Maserfelth was except that the present site of St.Oswalds Well at Hermitage Green was include. in this region as the spot where Oswald died during the battle and many towns in this area wer. known as "in Makerfield" up to the last century. The mysterious location of the battle was recorde. in 1170 AD as 'Macefen / Masefen' and in 1260 AD as 'le Masefen', thought to come from th. ancient Welsh/Celtic 'Maes-y-ffin' meaning 'the field at the boundary' or 'Mag-er' (Gaelic) and 'feld (Saxon) meaning 'the great cultivated plain'.

Oswald fell mortally wounded during the battle and clawed at the ground with his right han. as he died (possibly searching for his sword) and water began to rise from the spot which was the. visited as a sacred well with great healing properties for the next 1450 years. The resulting hol. created by pilgrims removing soil (Bede states that "a pit as deep as a man was formed") was fitte. with three stone steps and stone sides, one stone at the back of the well (now obscured) carved wit. the Christian letters I.H.S. (from the Latin for Jesus's name).

This well lies in a cow field, fenced off, at **OW** on the map on a sharp bend in the A573 Golborne Road at Hermitage Green. The land belongs to Woodhead Farm whicl sits on the top of the field rise and permission should be gained here before visiting the well.

Oswald's story, however, does not end with his death. As the Winwick cross arm shows, Penda ordered Oswald's body to be taken back to Mercia, nailed upside down by the feet to a tree and the arms and head cut off and set up on stakes at Oswestry. Some accounts have the body of Oswald completely cut into many pieces but the trunk is generally held to have been disemboweled then buried. At this point an eagle is said to have swooped down and carried off Oswald's right arm. At the spot where it dropped the arm, not far from the tree, another healing well bubbled from the ground, as it still does in its restored form at Oswestry today just off the B4579 to Telford.

ST. OSWALD'S WELL, OSWESTRY, 1870 - 1880.

Even the body parts of Oswald were said to heal - so Oswald's brother and successor Oswig (Oswin or Oswine) marched his army down to Oswestry in 643 AD and collected the remains, burying the head under the watchful eye of St.Aidan at Bardenaye, Lindisfarne and the arms at Bambrough.

The Celtic practice of venerating (worshipping) the head is legendary and the Celtic 'cult of the head' was known to be very strong in Northern Britain - an observation which helps to explain the next episode in Oswald's body story.

From Lindisfarne the head there was taken to Gloucester Abbey by the sister of King Edward the Elder. At a later date a head ended up in St.Cuthbert's grave in Durham while another head was displayed in a niello shrine at Hildesheim.

The right arm ended up in a silver shrine at Bamburgh and the left in the posession of Wulstan at Worcester. Yet another arm with healing powers found its way to Peterborough where King Stephen and many other nobles visited it. This is not impossible considering arms are made up of two parts and the Winwick cross carving of the dismembering already shows an absence of hands - destination unknown!

Beyond the death and break-up of King Oswald's body, other associated items became venerated *in true Celtic tradition. The stake on which his head had been impaled became a relic and a fragment of it cured a monk of the plague when he drank water in which the fragment had been soaked. Meanwhile, at Bardenaye, the water used to wash Oswald's bones had been poured away in a corner and dirt taken from this spot was used to cure those "possessed of devils". More of this water has been spilled on a stone pavement and dust swept up from here was dried, collected in a little bag, kept in a box and later used to cure an epileptic.*

Bede records that the faith of King Oswald also won through in the end with Penda converting to Christianity in 653 AD and, legend has it, that this is comemmorated by the two Celtic crosses at Sandbach in Cheshire. Penda may have actually been converted at Sandbach. Penda's son Peada later married a daughter of the Christian King Oswiu of Northumbria and Penda's daughter Cyneburga married a son of the same King.

In 655 AD King Penda was killed at the ripe old age of 79 and in 697 AD the bones of Oswald's trunk were exhumed by the Queen of Mercia and carried to Bardney (Lincs.) from where King Alfred's daughter Aethelflaed, the lady of the Mercians, collected them and brought them to Gloucester in about 918 AD. Another stray bone is recorded as arriving at York Cathedral where it remains as a relic to this day.

SANDBACH CROSSES 1870 - 1880.

Other than St.Oswald's Well, the most notable ancient well remaining of the 19 wells shown on the 1953 O.S. map is the Spa Well at **SW** on the map. Access can be gained down Arbury Lane and then across the field on a short farm track but visitors may be a little disappointed. In a rare privately-produced book, *Legends Of Old Lancashire*, this "only volcanic spring in Warrington" is shown flowing from a carved stone gargoyle's face into a pool. After the book was produced in 1952 the well was capped by the Water Authority and became one of four wells known as the Winwick bore hole (all shown as **W** on the map) which now supply drinking water to the local area. The gargoyle has gone - another vanishing carved stone!

Nature sometimes finds a way and a walk past the brick water board tower over the ancient well to the end of the wood will reveal that spring water still surfaces in quite large quantities to feed the Spa Brook and Arbury Pits.

Interesting to note in this area are the names of Arbury Farm and Arbury Pits, 'Arbury' usually meaning 'earth fortification'. Two other examples in Hertfordshire and Cambridgeshire are both sites of Roman military camps - which leads nicely into the tales of the Winwick pig.

Also of note is the Spa Well House to the east which is said to have belonged to Captain John Smith, the captain of H.M.S. Titanic when it sank.

OTHER WINWICK MYSTERIES

THE WINWICK PIG

Back again to the curious story of the Winwick pig. In the book form of the magazine *Notes And Queries* published by Bell and Daldy of Fleet Street in 1859, the following local tradition was recorded under 'Sites Of Buildings Changed':

FEEDING PIGS

"The foundation of the church, then, was laid where the founder had directed, and the close of the first day's labour showed the workmen had not been idle, by the progress made in the building. But the approach of night brought to pass an event which utterly destroyed the repose of the few inhabitants around the spot. A pig was seen running hastily to the site of the new church; and as he ran he was heared to cry or scream aloud 'We-ee-wick, We-ee-wick, We-ee-wick!' Then, taking up a stone in his mouth, he carried it to the spot sanctified by the death of St.Oswald, and thus employing himself through the whole night, succeeded in removing all the stones which had been laid by the builders.

"The founder, feeling himself justly reproved for not having chosen that sacred spot for the site of his church, unhesitatingly yielded to the wise counsel of the pig. Thus the pig not only decided the site of the church, but gave name to the parish. In support of this tradition, there is the figure of a pig sculpted on the tower of the church, just above the western entrance."

From the Celtic point of view this legend is interesting in that the pig or boar is, without doubt, the ultimate cult animal of the Celts having the greatest representational popularity in many contexts from Celtic helmet crests, coins and artifacts to actual food remains found in burials dating back before 500 BC. One of two bronze boars from the Celtic period found in Ireland also appears to have a bell round its neck like the representation on the Winwick church tower, and finds of various Celtic bells are also common.

As has been said, the Romans held the boar in honour as the god 'Moccus' ('Pig') equated with Mercury and it was the ensign of the Twentieth Legion who crossed the Mersey and marched past Winwick heading for the North between 71 and 74 AD, later

possibly being stationed there. If the origins of the stone Celtic/Christian church building lie in the pig story then the pig would be the traditional supernatural animal linked to Celtic kingly and Roman military status, and perhaps this also associated it with Arthur's visit or the death of St.Oswald. The pig on the tower faces the setting sun and it may be significant that King Arthur's shield (on which it is said to have appeared) was named 'WYNEBGWRTHUCHER' meaning 'Face Against Evening' in the Irish tale of 'Culhwch And Olwen' which was circulating about the date 1325 AD, shortly before the tower was constructed.

Having died at the site of the well, Oswald's complete body may have rested at the holy mound of Winwick, for the last time where the church now stands, before being transported to Oswestry for dismembering and public display by Penda.

It is said that the original church site was to be either on lower ground further down the hill or (more probably) close to St.Oswald's well in Hermitage Green, but that the pig carried the stones over High Fields to the Winwick mound - which may refer to the actual fact that an ancient quarry existed just North of Wood Head Farm before the building of the M6 motorway, from which foundation stones could have been taken. As a side note, the name 'Hermitage Green' is thought to be derived from the residence of an Augustinian Hermit Friar (Black Friar) sent from Warrington Friary to collect alms from Pilgrims to St.Oswald's Well in medieval times and 'Hermit House' was the name given on the 1934 large scale O.S. map to the buildings on the opposite side of the road to Woodhead Farm and the stone quarry, close to the well.

The 'Christian founder' of the church mentioned in the 'Pig Legend' could have been Oswig or St.Aidan and the monks of Lindisfarne between 648 and 651 AD. (At which date Oswig was killed at Gilling in Yorkshire by his cousin King Oswy and St.Aidan died a fortnight later of grief). St.Aidan's emblem is another Celtic 'animal of the hunt', the stag.

Another possible founder was King Alfred's daughter Ethelflaed during the 10th century (900 AD), who moved Oswald's remains to Gloucester and was a patron of churches and builder of forts in this area including one at Warburton.

Looking at the actual pig carving itself; the Haydock (later Legh) chapel had been constructed as a separate chapel in 1330 AD (the Haydock family 'Motte' still exists at the top end of Newton Lake next to the M6 motorway). The church tower which displays the pig carving facing the setting sun was then constructed by Sir Gilbert de Haydock and

Sir Gilbert de Southworth (the arms of whom are on the tower just below the battlements over the clock) in 1358 AD.

If the pig carving was always originally part of this tower structure, another not-so-ancient explanation for its presence there may apply. The church is dedicated to St.Oswald and St Anthony (or Antony) who lived in Egypt and the Red Sea region from 251 AD to 356 AD. He was a hermit and one story tells how he carried a piglet with a bell round its neck with him for some time begging scraps for it to eat. Eventually when people heard the bell they would get ready with scraps for the pig then, when the pig had become a fat adult, St.Anthony killed it and gave a great feast for the poor of the region. St.Anthony also used his bell to drive out evil spirits and was said to have "trampled on the wallowing pig", symbol of the lower passions of mankind. This is most likely the 'true story' behind this medieval pig emblem. The carving is on the tower next to the niche which has always held a statue of St.Anthony (the original was destroyed in the Civil War being replaced in 1973 along with another of King Oswald situated to the left).

Or could it be that it really does somehow represent the legendary Puck, Peg, Pich, Pick or Pix - the phantom Goblin church builder of Antiquity? Another local Victorian superstition claimed that the 'chained hog' was the resemblance of a monster in former ages, which prowled over the neighbourhood, inflicting injury on man and beast, and could only be restrained by the subduing power of the sacred edifice - a Saxon's memory of Arthur perhaps?

The Winwick Knight

It is interesting to make mention of the extremely rare drinking vessel discovered in Winwick churchyard in about 1840. It was made in the shape of a knight riding his horse and dating back to early 1100 AD - just after the Norman conquest. The terracotta vessel is broken, has many parts missing and is quite poorly produced in a primitive style but can still be compared to the Norman knights dressed for jousting depicted on other artifacts.

Unusual features of this knight include the high-sided saddle which resembles those used at the time in Asia and by the Celts, and a horse's breast plate made up of 'lozenge' shaped panels of mail - the 'lozenge' being a very ancient sacred and Druidic shape dating back to before 1800 BC. The absence of stirrups and the high-sided saddle may be significant as this combination would allow a soldier to be sufficiently firmly mounted to swing a weapon on horseback without stirrups. In the fourth century (300-400 AD) men so equipped, CATAPHRACTI were used by the Roman army (who never used stirrups) and it has been suggested that King Arthur was trained as a Celtic cataphractus.

Close examinations have led to the conclusion that the knight is made from local clay originating in the area around Sutton, near St.Helens. This is sufficiently close to Wigan ('Wiggin') for the vessel to represent the legendary activities of King Arthur and his knights in this area five hundred years earlier and re-told in stories by the Norman 'conteurs' or 'bards'.

Apparently, another later example of this type of vessel was found in Leadenhall Street Warrington before 1840, but no information is presently available on this find. The Winwick knight vessel is still on show in Warrington Museum.

The Winwick Treasure

During the long existence of the church at Winwick, large sums have been donated, especially during the medieval period, yet not a trace of the gold and silver artifacts and finery associated with such ancient ecclesiastical foundations has ever been found. It was noted in early times that Winwick was "one of the richest livings in England" and in 1835 it was estimated at £7000.00 a year with £3000.00 of that sum in tithes, as well as ownership of the "whole township of Winwick except half an acre of land belonging to the free school". (*History Of Lancashire*: *'Hundred Of West Derby - Winwick Parish'* by E.Baines).

Silver dating from after the Tudor period and a few items sold at auction are accounted for and held in a bank vault, but no record exists of anything more. Even Cromwell is not recorded as looting the church during his stay at the 'White Horse Inn' which is now the village Post Office, while he stabled his horses there and in the church (which had no pews at that time).

Searches have been made. The medieval vaults below the Gerrard Chapel were opened this century and briefly searched, but this revealed only the appropriate ancient

lead coffins stacked in their places. A door has been found 'bricked up' in the tower which appears to lead inside one of the buttresses but cannot be opened due to the listed status of the structure and the age of the closing brickwork. Is this the secret hiding place of the vanished medieval treasures, or were they already gone forever in the days before Cromwell? We may never know.

The Winwick Broad Oak

The winter of 1850 had been typical for Northern England and the locals at Winwick looked longingly forward to the arrival of spring. It was February, only ten days before St.Valentine's Day, when farmers returned home complaining of the gale force winds that had begun to lash the fields that day.

Before the 4th of February ended, the great and ancient Celtic 'Broad Oak' tree had become a victim of the onslaught and fallen after standing for well over a thousand years. So old and 'long standing' had this tree been that the acorn from which this ancient symbol of England grew may well have rooted on the very day that Oswald fell in battle!

The tree used to stand in a field behind the old school rooms and the Swan Pub, and was used as a canopy over a victory party for Sir Phipps Hornby on 26th August 1811 on his return following a naval victory over the French and Italian fleets at the battle of Lissa (1811). The Italian ship's flag is still displayed on the inside church wall to the right of the bell tower, although the surrounding 'frill' has decayed away.

After the gale, local residents were so grieved over the loss of the ancient Celtic Oak that it was made into four heavy wooden benches which still exist in the Gerrard Chapel in Winwick church to this day.

THE 'BROAD OAK' FROM A SKETCH OF 1836.

BEFORE LEAVING WINWICK

This brings us to our present millenium of mysteries which do not fall within the bounds set for this series of books.

The Knights Templar came to Winwick and left their shields on the ceiling bosses (angels) of the Legh Chapel. Sir Peter Legh's brass depicts him with his monk's attire over armour as late as 1455-1527 AD when King Henry VII stayed at 'Wonwick' (1495 AD).

An interesting but yet undocumented episode in local history stands 'written in bricks and mortar' in the form of Delph

THE STEPS INTO 'THE DELPH'.

THESE PHOTOS SHOW THE FRONT (ABOVE) AND REAR (BELOW) OF DELPH FARM PRIOR TO
THE RESTORATION OF THE BUILDING IN SUMMER 1998.
NOTE THE DATE STONE (1637) BELOW THE APEX OF THE ROOF ON THE PHOTO BELOW.
THE INTERIOR DOOR PANELS ARE SHOWN ON THE NEXT PAGE.

Farm. Built in 1637, and surviving Cromwell's visit to the area, it remains largely unchanged in over 350 years and stands on Delph Lane opposite the slightly older Tudor Myddleton Hall which is not open to public view. Delph Farm has two wells (one original and one Victorian), an inglenook fireplace and a rare painted door brought over from Myddleton Hall which features scenes of a mill, woodland, a church and a strange building like a big hotel (but obviously much older - see photographs). The original servants' quarters in the attic of the main building were opened again this year to reveal untouched rooms with wattle and daub partitions and beams exactly as they were 300 years ago. Three generations of the Robinson family lived here until the last surviving lady of the family died this summer and now the building will be restored, with archaeological supervision, in 1998 to its full glory by the new owners.

Sadly the Delph, after which the area is named, was filled in about 50 years ago and only the sunken area next to the farm remains.

Royalists and Roundheads came in 1642-1648 AD in the

Civil War and legends of Oliver Cromwell abound. For example 'Cromwell's Cave' in the Delph next to the main gate into the Winwick hospital site. This legend has turned out to have erroneously developed out of the existence of a derelict Victorian ice house hidden in the trees (and now demolished by road widening for a new development). The Cromwellian troops did much damage to Winwick church when they visited in May 1643 AD and after the battle of Red Bank in August 1648 AD. Later, in September 1665 AD, the diarist Roger Lowe found the unburied head of a trooper, borrowed a spade and buried it on a local farm (which was fortunate as King Charles II passed through Winwick around this time after a visit to Bryn) - but the ghostly armies supposedly still fight to this day in the surrounding fields.

Even now new legends are being written - like the day over thirty ice rings (similar to crop circles) appeared on the lake next to Myddleton Hall on the frosty 8th and 9th January 1997. Ice rings remain unexplained and this is probably the largest concentration of them ever recorded on one site.

D.J. Freke/Warrington Museum

THIS IS THE ONLY AERIAL PHOTOGRAPH OF THE SOUTHWORTH HALL BARROW (CROFT)
EXCAVATIONS OF 1980 TO HAVE BEEN TAKEN. THIS ENTIRE SITE HAS NOW BEEN SAND
QUARRIED AWAY.

CROFT AND CULCHETH

The time has come to finally move on. Take Myddleton Lane (the 'Eastern avenue' off the Winwick mound) out of Winwick towards Culcheth and it will lead down the ley line towards Croft where it becomes Southworth Lane as it passes the ancient Southworth Hall over the M6 motorway.

In the fields to the right may have been the burial mound at **7** on the map and in the field to the left, between the motorway and the hall itself, was sited the significant burial mound mentioned in the previous Winwick chapter as barrow **2**. While this site had been observed and recorded and a bronze 'palstave' type axe recovered from the area - nothing could have prepared the archaeologists for what followed when the site was fully excavated.

A PAGAN SACRED SITE - IN USE OVER 1500 YEARS

In 1980 a rescue archaeological unit from Liverpool University moved into the field to dig a barrow threatened by sand quarrying and came up with a suprising set of results which remained hidden in the soil of ages - and then for 18 years in the dusty archives of various Museums - until now.

It became quickly apparent that the archaeologists had unearthed a very ancient burial complex built in three obvious phases, followed by a pre-conquest (pre-Norman) cemetery. I will deal with their discoveries in carbon 14 date order, remembering that most dates this method gives are plus or minus 80 years either way.

1. THE PIT

The earliest feature detected at the site was an enigmatic and detached pit 6ft 4ins by 4ft 9ins by 1ft deep (2m x 1.5m x 300mm) filled with burnt cobblestones and charcoal dating back as far as 2140 BC. Stranger was the fact that the stones had not been burnt in the pit but brought from somewhere else and buried there!

One broken Bronze Age urn was recovered from this pit but no bones to indicate a burial. No solution for the presence or use of this pit has yet been forthcoming. It is a complete mystery! 51 feet (16m) to the south the next set of features were discovered.

2. THE FIRST MOUND

In 1740 BC a mound 38ft (12m) in diameter was raised with a steep-sided, flat-bottomed ditch about 4ft 9ins (1.5m) wide and 2ft 8ins (800mm) deep. Just off-centre the archaeologists discovered an oval pit 11ft 1ins by 8ft 1ins (3.5m x 2.5m) and more than 3ft 2ins (1m) deep, flat bottomed and very steep-sided.

In the sand in the middle of this pit was a slot 2ft 4ins wide by 2ft 4ins deep (700mm x 700mm) and as long as the original pit. The report of the dig reads:

"The almost vertical sides of this inner slot make it difficult to accept that it had been dug into the unconsolidated fill of the larger pit without some form of lining. Alternatively, it may be that the larger pit had been backfilled around some structure. No evidence for lining or structure was found."

Was this "slot" the site of a former standing stone or 'needle stone' erected during the Stone Age as a marker from the Winwick mound at **A** and then removed after a thousand years to accommodate a new breed of Bronze Age sacred site? The archaeologists also noted that the pit had a distinct north-east/south-west alignment.

D.J. Freke/Warrington Museum

Three burials and another small pit were found from this period randomly dotted on the mound and ditch. One burial deserves a mention as the decorated pottery rim found represents the only discovery of a biconical urn of the early Bronze Age in Cheshire and is several centuries older than most other known examples, most of which are not decorated (which the Croft rim is).

Early date finds show that man developed in an unbroken chain from stone to bronze and to iron at Winwick and Croft. This early mound was levelled and the ditch filled in about 1600 BC to make way for another second structure - some form of wooden building!

3. The Shaman's Sanctuary

A triple ring of stakes was driven into the levelled first mound in three concentric ovals measuring 4ft 9ins (1.5m inside ring), 12ft 8ins (4m middle ring) and 20ft 7ins (6.5m outer ring) and supporting a structure which only survived to be found by archaeologists as a mass of charcoal including some wattle and wider strips of wood like thin planks. The standing stone, if it existed, would have been removed by this point as the new wooden stakes cut into the now empty and filled-in central pit.

Was this an early Bronze Age religious 'church' of some kind, a sort of 'Shaman's Sanctuary' like those still constructed by the American Plains Indians? Was it an observatory like Woodhenge near Avebury, Wiltshire (with a roof but open walls), where the ancients spent long nights of star-gazing and debate? It remains as another Croft mystery.

To add to this the wooden structure was mysteriously burnt down in about 1520 BC before construction of the second mound.

4. The Second Mound

The second mound (third structure) was a massive 76ft wide (24m) and more than 8ft (2.5m) high, roughly sited over the first mound and having a ditch 3ft 2ins wide by 3ft 10ins deep (1m x 1.2m). So large was this mound that the turf used to build it would have had to be brought in from the surrounding area.

D.J. Freke/Warrington Museum

Nine, possibly ten, burials and a small bone knife hilt ('pommel') were found in this mound. There were two with urns, two with small accessory vessels, one with both and five with neither - but mysteriously none of these occupied the centre of the mound and all were inserted into the mound after its construction was completed.

D.J. Freke/Warrington Museum

The burial with both an urn and an accessory vessel deserves a mention as the vessel had been buried at a later date to the urn but placed exactly over the middle of the older upright collared urn. The chevron markings on both are so similar that they suggest some direct relationship between both burials, the first of which must have been marked on the surface in order to be relocated. Was this father and son, husband and wife, human and sacrifice? We may never know. This burial is quite unique and dates to about 1440 BC (as do the others in mound two) and the use of the wheel-cross motif on the base of both accessory vessels is worthy of note for its age although the ancient significance is lost. (See photos P. 54)

The pattern of burials found in the second mound also suggests a plan to their location possibly relating to alignments. I will quote the final summary from the report published in the *Journal Of The Chester Archaeological Society*, Volume 70 for 1987-88 written by D.J. Freke and R. Holgate:

"Seven of the surviving cremations fall into two groups opposite one another, joined by the axis of the first phase central pit. This axis, if it is intentional, is the more remarkable because it indicates the persistence of an alignment from the earliest constructional period, when the central pit was dug, filled in and covered with a sand mound, through to the latest detectable Bronze Age use of the site after another mound had been erected over the top of the first.

"If this alignment did persist for c.300 years it suggests that some sort of long-term marker in the environment was being used. No obvious marker, such as a skyline notch, exists now in the landscape. No search has been made for a celestial alignment, which would be in the region of 45 degrees east of north."

The account continues,

"A possible secondary alignment, comprising the four other cremations and all five Bronze Age pits, exists at right-angles to the first. Only two of the north-east -

south-west burials are without a pot, whereas only one of the four north-west - south-east burials has an accompanying pot, the crudest of the collection.

"If the two alignments are accepted, then it seems reasonable to consider the north-east - south-west one as the principal one on the grounds of the pit axis, the greater number of burials, and the number of pots accompanying them."

As a final note to finds made in the mounds, most surviving bone fragments were adult with some identifiable as male but the acid soil had destroyed almost all traces of bones over the whole site. Many flint implements were found in the area but, whilst the arrow heads were clearly Bronze Age, there was no evidence that the rest were related to either of the mounds although Stone Age man had certainly been active in the area.

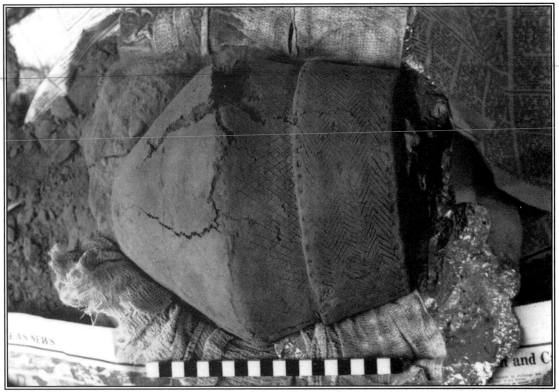

D.J. Freke/Warrington Museum

D.Longley in *Prehistoric Sites In Cheshire,* published in 1979, mentions an urn found at Southworth which may relate to this site or the "eastern barrow" mentioned in 1860 by Dr.Kendrick - but the urn has now been lost and no other details are available.

A CELTIC SACRED SITE - IN USE OVER 1000 YEARS

For the next two thousand years between 1400 BC and 600 AD, the development of the area can only be surmised as that dark 'Celtic' silence slips into the historic record once again.

It is known that burials began again on the site in the form of normal graves (not Bronze Age Urn cremations) at some point during this period, and the archaeologists

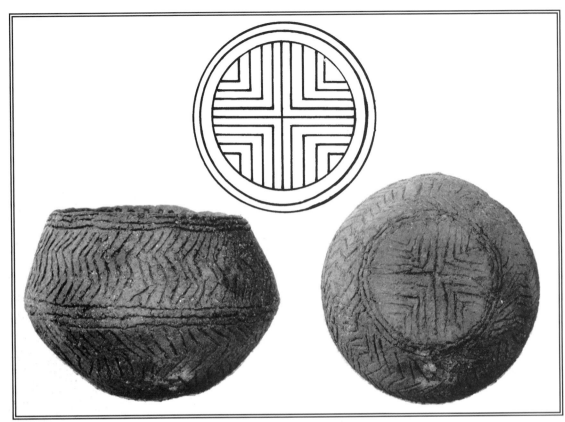

uncovered at least 819 of these burials in the trench surrounding the mounds, cut into the soft sandstone. It also appeared that burials took place actually on the mound which would increase this number to over 1200 and burials also stretched away across the field in all directions to as many as 2-3000 graves. At the time of the excavation some graves were found that could have been as late as the reformation period when Catholics were afforded shelter at Southworth.

No cemetery boundary was ever found and the enigmatic alignment from the original mound-pit continued into this period with most graves pointing 45 degrees west of north. Although two phases of burial were common over most of the site, a strangely high concentration of graves also seemed to have gathered in the vicinity of the original stone-filled pit from 2140 BC, with as many as four indistinguishable phases of burial crowded into a blur. Why? No one knows.

The site showed no clue to the position of a chapel, boundary or footpath but the fact that the burials show some degree of planning might show a date of Roman or later as such cemeteries as this are known in other areas of Roman and post-Roman Christian activity which did not succumb to early Anglo-Saxon settlement and the associated influences.

D.J. Freke/Warrington Museum

It has been surmised from a pattern of gaps in the burials that a wooden building 12ft 8ins wide x 25ft 6ins (4m x 8m) may have stood on the site but, like wooden coffins, only dirt discolouration remained.

A CHRISTIAN SACRED SITE - IN USE OVER 1800 YEARS

The archeological report suggests from the evidence that the cemetery remains are either

A] an early Christian one from the orientation of heads to the west, no grave goods and communal long-term burial rather than cremation, or

B] that it may be of much later Germanic origin based on the use of a burial mound as the centre point and a single burial which had a stone either side of the head - a practice continued up to the late 11th century.

Of course the cemetery could span the whole of the Celtic period into modern times and there are no other indications at this time to support the 'Germanic origin' theory.

There was certainly a chapel in the township of Southworth in 1292 AD and the field in which the burials lie was recorded as 'Further Chapel Flatt' on a map as late as 1841, quite a coincidence if this had nothing to do with the cemetery. But still the greatest mystery remains, why did the pattern of the cemetery stay the same for 3500 years from the Pagan into to the Christian era and what do the structures represent?

As a last word I will quote again from the the *Chester Archaeological Journal* No 70:

> *"Though such evidence as it yields looks middle or even late Saxon, the Winwick (Southworth Hall) cemetery could well have spanned the whole Dark Age period. Viewed thus it provides crucial evidence of pre-Conquest activity in an area singularly lacking in British and Anglo-Saxon remains."*

Sadly, this site has now been utterly swept away by sand quarrying.

MORE BRIEF TALES OF CHURCHES AND CHAPELS

Moving on down Southworth Lane into Croft, at an area known as Smithy Brow, turn left down the ancient single track Dam Lane. The Winwick ley comes through here just below Cockshot Bridge and a flat Bronze Age 'palstave' axe head was found here just after the turn of the century. This may indicate that the 'eastern mound' mentioned by Dr.Kendrick and marked as **7** on the map, could have existed in this area.

Three wells now capped by the Water Authority link this lane with the Spa Well at Winwick forming the Winwick Bore Hole (MAP MARKED W). A brick well-cap structure the same as the one over Spa Well appears in a garden to the right just as you leave Dam lane. Here turn left onto Step House Lane and, to the left, is Deacons Farm and Deakins Cottage, both of which echo their possible ecclesiatical origins. Take the first right down New Lane and, after about a mile, a small Victorian cemetery devoid of its chapel will appear on the left. This is the second of the series of 'dislocated' cemeteries mysteriously found in this area for a variety of reasons (the first being Southworth Hall).

This cemetery is part of the old original burial ground of the Independent Methodist Chapel built in 1817 which had been demolished by the 1870s after burials began in earnest at Croft Parish Church (a hill mound site on the Winwick ley) built in 1832-33 and just up the road.

Another older cemetery exists further to the East but is an optional detour from our desired route. This is the site of the old Thomas Risley United Reformed Church (Chapel) which was demolished to build the M62 motorway and can be reached by continuing to

the end of New Lane/Cross Lane, turning right onto Warrington Road (A574) and taking the first right just over the M62 into Cross Lane South. Sadly no ancient cross now exists on Cross Lane. Down at the bottom of this short cul-de-sac the cemetery appears behind railings on the right.

A notable feature of this tiny burial ground is the tomb of the church founder, the Rev. Thomas Risley himself. His family was named after the area Risley (formerly Ryselegh, Risselley or Riselegh) which is thought to mean 'twigs or brushwood' but the name only dates back to about 1284 AD. His tombstone reads:

**Here interrd the body of the Revd Thomas Risley MA Oxford,
he left the Church of England in 1662 and built Risley Chapel in 1707
where he often attended up to his death, he died in 1716 aged 86 years.
THE RIGHTEOUS SHALL BE IN EVERLASTING
REMEMBERANCE. PSALM CXII.6.**

Back to our original route in Croft. At the small cemetery on New Lane turn left into Lady Lane and go up the hill to a right hand bend where Croft Church and rectory appear on the right. At this bend, an old iron gate to the left closes off the course of an old road which formed part of the ley line from Winwick on which sits Croft Church on a small raised hill. Information about the previous use of this church site does not appear to exist and the church is an entirely early Victorian structure surrounded by a small cemetery still in use. There is little doubt that something ancient would have stood on this hill but further investigation may not now be possible.

The name 'Croft' originates from the Anglo-Saxon for a 'field adjacent to a dwelling' (other examples exist in Herefordshire, Lincolnshire and Yorkshire). This

The church at Croft.

obviously implies that the area between Winwick and Culcheth was primarily given over to farming as long ago as 500 AD and that there were quite a few farming families living in early houses in the area, probably on the outskirts of the city at Winwick.

Celtic rule was maintained for almost two hundred years longer in the Mersey Valley than in areas of south and south-eastern England, and when the wave of Anglo-Saxon settlers finally reached the area in the early 7th century (600-700 AD), there is every reason to suppose that the initial numbers were relatively few. However, in a wonderfully poetic manner the Celtic writer Gildas described the invading Angles and Saxons as "a fire from the East which burned from sea to sea" and "did not die down until, consuming almost all the island that stood above ground, it licked the Western Ocean with its red and savage tongue." These new settlers cut back local forests to form new villages and Culcheth as a larger settlement area may well have been one of these.

Continue up Lady Lane to the T-junction at Little Town and turn right for Culcheth village.

WHAT'S IN A NAME?

If you look at the South Lancashire region of any Saxon map of England you will soon find the position of 'Calchuth' or 'Celchyth' and there is little doubt that the present Culcheth area is intended. In these early maps and deeds the name is also written as 'Kilcheth', 'Kylchith' or 'Kilshaw' and is thought to derive from the Celtic 'at the edge of a wood', 'back wood' or 'retreat in a wood' - although the less likely Anglo-Saxon alternative 'shoe-shaped heath' has also been suggested.

Other British Celtic names from the 7th century (600-700 AD) to survive in the area are 'Haydock' (name derived from 'hedges of oak' or 'oaks in the hedges'), 'Makerfield', 'Glazebury', 'Eccles', 'Dunham-on-the-Hill', 'Dunham Massey' and 'Kenyon'. Names of earlier origin, with the Anglian settlers of 570 AD, are: 'Dumplington', 'Partington', 'Carrington', 'Oughtrington', 'Altrincham', 'Warburton' and 'Warrington', which all have Anglian structure (although many are from even earlier roots).

SAXTON'S MAP OF LANCASHIRE 1577

While on the subject of special names, two local farms bear the distinctive 'barrow' element indicating the presence of Bronze Age burial mounds or similar features in former times. The first is at Twiss Green north of Culcheth, the name 'Twiss' meaning "the place where two streams meet" - which they do; thus the 'Green' of the village formerly sat on a tongue of land between two streams. Leatherbarrow Farm sits just north of this ancient village of Twiss next to the old hospital site at **11** on the map. The farm name is interesting in that some Celtic tumulus burials have been found contained in leather bags instead of clay urns, hence, possibly, the name 'leather' barrow. A rare example of this type of burial has been found in the area just over the Mersey in 1987, accompanied by seven flints and a riveted dagger. This 'bag burial' was found at Fairy Brow, Little Bollington, and carbon 14 dated to about 1485 BC contemporary with finds in Croft.

The second farm is Netherbarrow Farm further north east, about a mile from Glazebury towards the East Lancashire Road (A 580) bordering on Bedford Moss. In old English 'nether' meant 'distant' or 'furthest' and this is the last reference to 'barrow' in any local place names before reaching the outskirts of Manchester where all evidence from this period has long been covered up by development. If viewed from the mound at Winwick both of these barrows would be on the line of a minor solar stand-still, but from the mound complex discovered at Southworth Hall, Croft, they sit on the Midsummer sunrise, both important ancient alignments from significant local sites.

The only evidence of Bronze Age activity in the form of items found at Culcheth (that I can locate at present) is a large bronze 'palstave' axe head dating back to the middle Bronze Age that was found in 1965 and is presently on show in Warrington Museum. This magnificent example may well have been dislocated from a former burial mound or deposited in water as an offering but no background information is presently available.

EVIDENCE OF DRUIDS AND PRIESTS

On the way into Culcheth, just over the old railway bridge and the linear park, Wigshaw Lane passes the lower end of Hob Hey Lane to the left and this road is of great interest from an ancient linguistic viewpoint.

A 'Hob' was an ancient country demon and a 'Hey' was an enclosure, often fenced and especially in forests. Do we have here the location of a "demon in the wooded clearing" - otherwise known as an ancient Pagan or Druidic 'grove'?

Culcheth would certainly have been on the edge of ancient English woodland (or even in the centre of a wood) in Celtic times, and the Celts were known to use old English forest groves for ritual and tribal assembly as well as holding the oak and other trees sacred. Oak boughs and mistletoe were found placed in an oak coffin burial in a tumulus at Gristhorpe near Scarborough in 1834 and several sacred wooden figures from the Celtic period have been found which could have been intended for use as statues in groves. This could easily have led to the 'Hob' legend, especially as the tribal Celtic god of Northern Britain was 'Cernunnos' who was depicted looking like a man/demon with horns.

At the top of Hob Hey Lane several Victorian properties are also named after woodland fauna on the 1928 O.S. map, including 'Laurel', 'Ivy' and 'Lime'.

Connected with local Druidic practices, it is also known that human sacrifice occured in the surrounding mossland areas with a male Celtic skull being recovered from the nearby Bedford and Chat Moss lands. The Chat Moss skull, found in 1958, dates back to 100-200 AD, placing it in the same time frame as the famous 'Lindow Man' sacrifice of Lindow Common, further into the mid-Cheshire mosslands. Close examination has revealed that this victim, known as 'Worsley Man', had suffered a ritual death similar to 'Lindow Man', having been hit on the head with a blunt instrument, garotted and then decapitated before being placed in the waters of the ancient bog. Interestingly, 42 bog bodies have so far been discovered in England and 20 in Ireland, with the earliest record of a Celtic bog burial being Irish.

At this point it is worth revealing an overall pattern found in ancient Celtic remains in the local mosslands as it adds considerably to the picture of the area which emerges from dark Celtic times. Essentially, the further east from Winwick you travel, the further into the realms of ancient Druids you go. From the city of Winwick the small villages and farms would have decreased until fields gave way to forests and then forests to dense marsh lands crossed by ancient tracks. These marshes formed a vast arc, a sort of 'mossland crescent', which reached south into Cheshire, to stop only at the stark, imposing ridge of Alderly Edge and Lindow Common. Contained in the northern part of this arc are the areas now called Rixton, Risley, Holcroft, Glazebrook, Bedford, Worsley and Chat mosslands.

Druids could sail from their headquarters in Anglesey, Wales or Ireland into the river Mersey as far as the ford and port at Warrington and then take smaller boats further up river and directly into their sanctuaries in the mosslands. They could also disembark and take the ancient roads and tracks via Winwick and the ley line systems that ultimately reached out beyond the mosslands to the Pennines.

THE BRONZE OX AND THE CAULDRON

In 1734 in "the parish of Croft" a Roman/Celtic bronze figure of an ox was found, followed in 1825 by the discovery of a bronze cauldron. The report of the ox discovery is given in *The History Of Lancashire* by H.Fishwick as follows:

> *"In 1734 the brazen metope of an ox was found on a bed of white sand in Risley, under a bed of peat soil five yards (4.7m) deep. This ancient piece of workmanship, thus singularly placed, is mentioned by Dr. Aikin (?), who describes it as three-quarters of an inch (2cm) by two inches and a half (6cm) between the horns."*

While the ox and cauldron have both been assigned a Roman identification primarily due to their estimated date, the Celtic and Druidic significance of such a find as a cauldron cannot be stressed too highly. Given the circumstances, it is highly unlikely that this item in particular was owned and used by a Roman. The bronze cauldron is the ultimate representation of Celtic shamanism, mystery and magic from which otherworldly life 'flowed' in legend, and cauldrons were often thrown into water as offerings by their Druid owners. The bronze ox was probably also an offering in connection with the prosperity of local cattle, although this find is quite unique.

Both of these items appear to have been deposited as offerings into mossland as the contemporary records regarding the finds say they came from below the peat levels. This would also place both finds close to the mosslands in the east of the ancient 'Parish of Croft', hence their appearance under this section on what is now the Culcheth/Risley area. Sadly, a precise location for both of these finds is lacking as with a fragment of a Roman Urn with a distinctive basket-weave pattern on the rim that was unearthed somewhere on the Risley Moss site during the late 1980s.

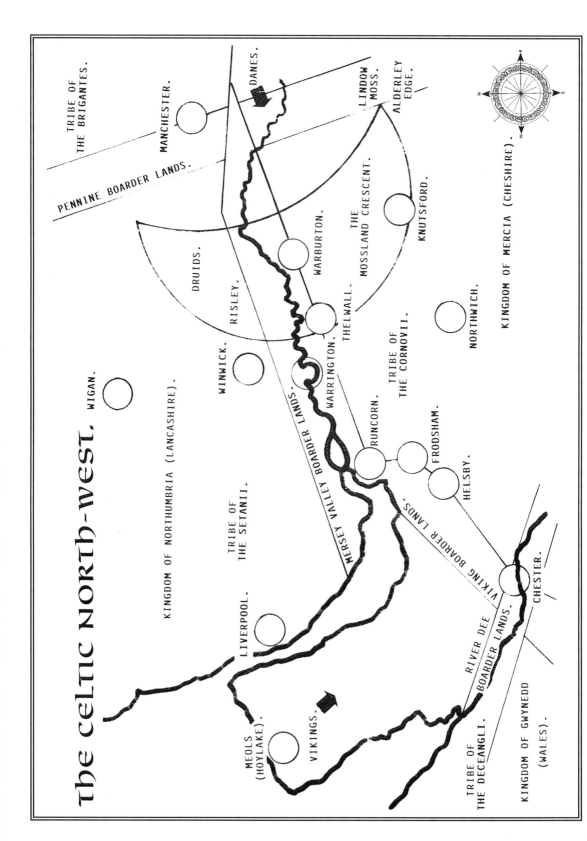

The Celtic North-West.

TRIBE OF THE BRIGANTES.

PENNINE BOARDER LANDS.

MANCHESTER.

DANES.

LINDOW MOSS.

ALDERLEY EDGE.

KNUTSFORD.

THE MOSSLAND CRESCENT.

WARBURTON.

DRUIDS.

RISLEY.

THELWALL.

NORTHWICH.

KINGDOM OF MERCIA (CHESHIRE).

WINWICK.

WARRINGTON.

TRIBE OF THE CORNOVII.

WIGAN.

KINGDOM OF NORTHUMBRIA (LANCASHIRE).

TRIBE OF THE SETANII.

RUNCORN.

FRODSHAM.

HELSBY.

MERSEY VALLEY BOARDER LANDS.

VIKING BOARDER LANDS.

CHESTER.

LIVERPOOL.

RIVER DEE BOARDER LANDS.

MEOLS (HOYLAKE).

VIKINGS.

TRIBE OF THE DECEANGLI.

KINGDOM OF GWYNEDD (WALES).

A further interesting tribal observation can be made regarding the mosslands. These areas found in Warrington's north-eastern sector (and covered by this book) would have been in the posession of the Celtic tribes known as the 'Brigantes'. One of this confederation were known as the 'Setanii' or 'Segantii' which means 'the dwellers in the water country'. Could this tribe have been centred on and served by the Druids from our own 'water country', the local mosslands?

The Mossland Crescent

Rixton, Risley and Holcroft mosslands lie in the ancient parish of Croft/Culcheth and have yielded some interesting finds so I will deal with these areas under this section and return to Risley later as part of Birchwood.

From the Stone Age period onwards, finds have been recorded in the 'Mossland Crescent'. A number of flints turned up during pipeline construction on Risley/Rixton moss in 1982 and a stone mace head shaped like a giant 'doughnut' designed to fit a shaft was found in top soil taken from Birchwood in 1985 (similar to one found 12 feet (3.5m) below ground at Bruche Hall, Haydock in 1841).

The North West Wetlands Survey published in 1997 by the Lancaster University archaeological department showed, by testing samples of the mossland at Rixton and Risley, that at least 15 woodland clearances and regenerations had taken place over the last 5000 years since Neolithic times (3000 BC). Cereal pollen appeared in the top 3ft 2in (1m) and hemp pollen (Cannabis type) in the top 4ft 9ins (1.5m). Could this have been the magical 'Druids' crop'? Actually hemp has many uses other than as a drug including rope and string manufacture, cloth, matting and food.

According to the report the mossland was also affected by four significant environmental changes with bogs and woodland on uplands in Neolithic times (3000 BC), a change to open dryer conditions in the Bronze Age (2000 BC), back to wetter conditions in the Iron Age (1000 BC) before the effects of farming and settlement arrived over the last 2000 years AD.

During the survey a small concentration of 6 various stone flints were found on the crest of a sandy ridge in the north west part of Rixton/Risley moss and classified as late Mesolithic or early Neolithic (between 6700 BC and 3200 BC), possibly the oldest man-made finds in the entire north-east sector of Warrington to date! Many more stray flints were then found scattered over the moss including some burnt flint flakes and mysterious flint nodules. The Wetlands Survey No 4, page 24 reads,

"More enigmatically a number of burnt flint nodules were also encountered. These could, perhaps, represent traces of some undefined prehistoric activity but might just as easily be the by-products of a recent industrial process."

Who knows? Another mystery similar to the pit of stones at the Southworth Hall mound in Croft. These stray flint finds were all classified at the later Neolithic to Bronze Age period from 3200 to 800 BC.

After the Druids chose to make the woodlands and mosslands their sacred home, the Celtic traditions gradually developed into Christian traditions and the history of Croft and Culcheth entered a new phase.

SAINTS AND SYNODS!

About a century and a half after the death of King Oswald at Winwick in 642 AD there was an administrative council held at 'Cealc-hythe', 'Calchuth' or 'Celchyth', which was then referred to as a "famous place"! The first mention comes in the Anglo-Saxon Chronicle and states that: "There was a great synod at Cloueshoh, and present were King Aethelbald of Mercia (716-757 AD), Archbishop Cuthbert (c.740 AD) and other learned men."

Following this the 'Legatine Council of Chalchyth' is recorded in the Anglo-Saxon Chronicle under 785 AD: "This year there was a 'contentious' or 'litigious' synod at Cealchythe, and Archbishop Jaenbryht (or Jaenberht) gave up some portion of his bishoprick; and Higebryht was elected by King Offa; and Egferth (Offa's son) was consecrated king." A king crowned at Culcheth!

The discoveries by Liverpool University Archaeologists in 1980, which point to a large Christian settlement in the area of Southworth Hall, and the associations of King Oswald at Winwick may help to explain the choice of the Culcheth area for this and future synods but these were probably not the actual sites chosen to host them, being too far west of the region named.

From 785-787 AD Pope Aidan I sent his representatives, George (Bishop of Ostia) and Theophylact (Bishop of Todi), to the synod with twenty Injunctions (or Articles) of behaviour expected of the British church and its membership. This was only the second Papal mission to England, the first being that of St.Augustine (or Austin) and his party who first arrived in Kent to evangelise in 596 AD, and the only Catholic Papal mission ever to reach the North of the country - and they came to Culcheth!

In 789 AD there was another synod at Celchyth, the business of which was purely to do with Mercia. Here King Offa of Mercia made grants to Rochester. In 793 AD, according to a more questionable charter, at a synod in Culcheth, King Offa made grants to St.Albans in the presence of a Mercian grantor and grantees. Two more charters are recorded in 796 AD, followed by a synod in 799 AD on Mercian matters and a Council in 816 AD devoted to the province of Canterbury.

THE LOST ABBEY OF CULCHETH

Obviously a monastic or administrative site of some significance existed at Culcheth in these later Celtic times, 700-900 AD (for example the existence of 'Old Abbey' farm moated site less than a mile to the south). But the location of the 'Great Synods Of Culcheth' which took place over a two hundred year period remains a complete mystery.

Excavations at Old Abbey Farm undertaken at the request of UK Waste Management Ltd. prior to the site being destroyed under a tip found the earliest settlement phase only dated back to the 13th century (1200-1300 AD) and that the name appeared quite recent in origin. No monastic remains of any kind were found at the site and certainly nothing 'Celtic', so the 'Old Abbey' had eluded searchers once again!

The Abbey would not have been located in the 'Newchurch' area either as this area derives its name from a church which burnt down with only the parish registers being saved. After thousands of years, perhaps the shadow of the Druid groves hidden in the dark, boggy woodlands had left a powerful, religious memory in the area which caused all future Christian generations to gravitate to the same general location in the mossland crescent east of Winwick at the once 'famous place' of Culcheth?

In 875 AD the Norsemen came to the area after sacking Northumbria between 792 and 793 AD, and the Danes followed by destroying Lindisfarne in 795 AD and, during King Alfred's building work on Chester in 894 AD, they raided there for two days signalling the arrival of more new visitors to the Warrington area. Chester and Warrington were then under attack from Norsemen and Danes up to Igimund's Norse attacks in 902-910 AD and the 'Abbey' may have been destroyed as long ago as this time. National peace was not attained again until the Normans brought it by force after 1066 AD

Seven hundred years after the synods of Culcheth, in his map of 1577, Saxton shows the Kilcheth (Culcheth) area to be surrounded by Ashton Chapel, Newton Chapel, Bryche (Bruche), Rysley (Risley), Holcroft, Chatmosse, Leghe (Leigh) with churches at Wynwick (Winwick) and Newchurch. North of Kilcheth and next to Ashton Chapel is the now vanished town of 'Byram'! Where did it go? Was it Bryn?

THE AREAS OF

GLAZEBROOK

WARBURTON

RIXTON

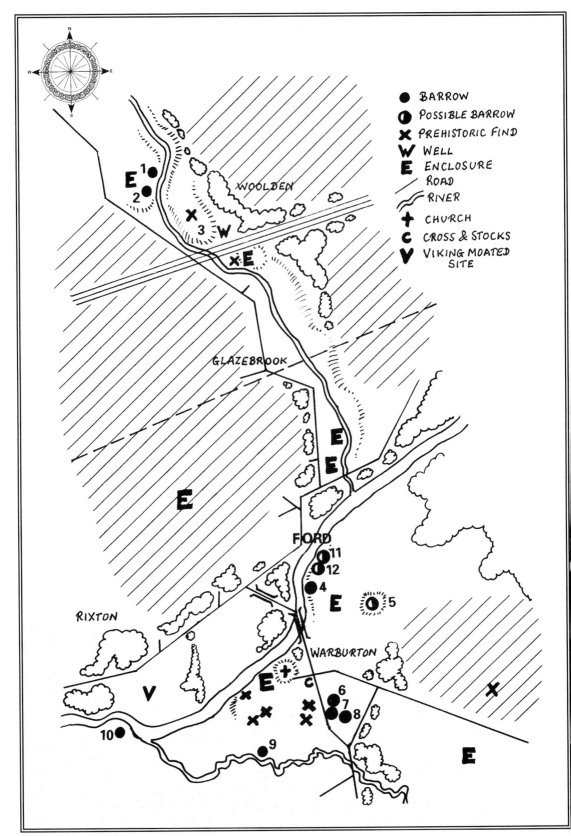

GLAZEBROOK

From the bottom end of Hob Hey Lane continue to drive into Culcheth down Wigshaw Lane and, at the first T-junction, turn right onto the B5207 Common Lane with Culcheth Village Green on the left. At the next T-junction turn left onto the A574 to Glazebury and drive past the High School on the left. Take the next right down the B5212 to Glazebrook. This leads on to Glazebrook Lane. Continue driving towards Glazebrook village and you will enter the realms of the Celtic Iron Age.

A SUMMER FLIGHT TO WOLF VALLEY

The sun is rising on a dry summer's morning as you fly your single-engine light aircraft along the length of the glittering Glazebrook, the name 'GLAZE' derived from the Celtic 'GLASTO' meaning "green/blue" or the Germanic 'GLASA' meaning "bright". As the shadows pick out forms in the ground below, you become aware that the tiny river valley along which the B5212 runs is littered with markings from ages gone by. Morning mist clears and, on closer inspection, this brief aerial survey reveals the following features.

As the road swings closer to the brook between Crow Wood and Little Woolden Hall you notice some adjacent circular crop marks which may be ditches from very ancient buildings or, more likely barrows (MAP NUMBERS **1** & **2**).

Next your eye is drawn to settlement markings at Great Woolden Hall just over the M62 before your plane flies south to two more markings opposite Mount Pleasant Farm and the Black Sheep Craft Centre. The first is a curvilinear mark which cuts off a small promontory jutting into the Glazebrook, another settlement possibility. The second is part of a double-ditched rectangular enclosure first found on photographs in 1984.

You land your plane by the Craft Centre and set out by car to investigate the markings by the M62 and the two Woolden Halls, the name 'WOOLDEN' being derived from the Old English 'WULF' meaning 'wolf' and 'DENU' meaning 'valley' hence 'WOLF VALLEY'.

Only the markings visible at Greater Woolden Hall have been excavated so far but with excellent results.

IRON AGE INDUSTRIAL REVOLUTION

The site was first discovered on aerial photographs in 1986 and excavations by Greater Manchester Archaeological Unit began in 1987 on the river terrace next to the M62 called 'Red Field', on the opposite side of the Glazebrook to the B5212.

G.M.A.U. Archive

TOP RIGHT IS A BELGIC TYPE POT. BOTTOM RIGHT THE BASE OF A LOCAL POT.
MIDDLE RIGHT IS THE 'RED FIELD' SITE OF THE EXCAVATION.

This was the first opportunity ever afforded to excavate a site of this type in the Greater Manchester area and it is still intended that these excavations should continue (as the opportunity arises) but so far, four main circular structures have been identified along with other interesting discoveries.

Two of the circular structures are 41ft 2ins-47ft 6ins (13-15m), one other circle is about 25ft 4ins (8m) and the smallest about 17ft 6ins (5m). The large quantity of pottery and timber finds suggest a date of use from a maximum range of about 800 BC to 200 AD. Radiocarbon dating confirmed one occupation from approximately the 100 BC period.

G.M.A.U. Archive.

THE RIGHT PHOTOS SHOW THE CIRCULAR HUT FEATURES AND THE LEFT PHOTOS SHOW THE OVERALL EXCAVATIONS AT WOOLDEN IN 1987.

When constructed these four structures were then protected by two ditches dug deeper than the level of the Glazebrook, both of which would have been filled with water to cut the site off from the rest of the land of similar height. Six pits were identified and three excavated, all of which showed signs of burning. Two had near-vertical sides and flat bottoms 6ft 2ins x 2ft 4ins x 1ft 3ins (1.9 x 0.74 x 0.4m), lined with large stones. This time these stones were burnt in the pits, not deposited from somewhere else.

A number of clay-lined features were also uncovered and interpreted as 'ovens'. One to the north-west consisted of two hand-depth clay 'bowls' about 3ft 2ins (1m) across. Another oval shaped single 'bowl' of similar size was found inside one of the big circular structures. All had once included structures made from stakes surrounding them.

A flint blade and over 3000 grams of pottery fragments have so far been recovered from the site and from the surrounding fields. Surface finds are mostly post-medieval with some Roman fragments but pieces actually dug up at the settlement fall into three distinct categories: A]. early hand-made, B]. Cheshire Stony Very Coarse Pottery (known as Cheshire Stony VCP) and C]. Romano-British wares from a later period.

Mike Nevell's report in volume 3 of *The Greater Manchester Archaeological Journal* (1987-88) concluded that,

"The quantity and quality of the finds has been surprising when compared to other similar sites excavated in the region. The identifiable prehistoric shards (pottery) represent the largest such close group excavated on a site of this type in the North-West."

He continues,

"The examples of Cheshire Stony VCP represent the most northerly find so far of this material. Indeed the only other occurrence of this pottery type in the region is at Beeston Castle in central Cheshire."

Cheshire Stony VCP is also the only known Late Prehistoric pottery to be produced in Cheshire, somewhere in the Nantwich-Middlewich area, and possibly used for the transportation of salt.

The report concludes that the site at Greater Woolden Hall had at least three phases of development (with a possible fourth in the Roman period now ploughed out and destroyed), the largest circular structures representing compounds made from wooden stakes, wattle and daub for industrial rather than domestic use. It would appear that the smallest 17ft 6ins (5m) structure was once an animal pen defined by a wooden stake wall. Possibly Celtic riders watered their horses here at Wolf Valley as they brought salt and other products north or possibly local pottery manufacturers traded goods made in their own 'ovens' from this collection of circular compounds - but they had not been alone in this 'Dark-Age' landscape.

THIS IRON AGE RECONSTRUCTION GIVES A VIVID IDEA OF A HUT FROM THIS PERIOD.

MORE MOUNDS AND WELLS

On the opposite side of the M62 to this site there is a long hill in front of Little Woolden Hall that was shown on the first edition of the one inch O.S. map for this area (produced between 1805 and 1873) as displaying a set of six standing stones, three in a line along the centre of the ridge terminating at three in a triangle next to the present M62. This arrangement is not unlike a very simplified version of those once found at the Bride Stones in Staffordshire (which were the remains of a very large long barrow dedicated to the burial of a Celtic Queen).

Two very large boulders which may have been dragged off this field still remain either side of the track next to Little Woolden Hall, which also sits on a very ancient square earth enclosure. The present owners report that many fragments of buildings older than the present hall, built in 1756, have been found during renovation.

An ancient oak, which could date back over a thousand years, still grows to the front left of the hall and a small circular 'grove' of more recent but very large trees has developed on a circular mound with a central depression located at the rear left corner of the hall. This may be a small depressed 'pond barrow' and any of the features observed at this site could indicate settlement here well before the Holcroft family developed the Woolden estates starting in 1595.

There was also a natural spring shown on the 1953 O.S. map which appears to be next to 'Keepers Cottage' in a gully by the little wood once called 'Woolden Clough' and later 'Great Woolden Wood'. This is just off the hillside to the east on the edge of Great Woolden Moss (formerly part of Chat Moss). The wood has been reduced to a very small collection of trees by the building of the M62 and the spring is now close to a private garden, but any future archaeological activity in the area should take account of its existence. It may well represent an undiscovered Celtic 'sacred well' and the ancient water source for all the settlements in this area (of which more have recently been discovered on Chat Moss dating back over 7000 years but outside the area covered in this book).

All the Little Woolden sites are private and any visitors are asked to report to Little Woolden Hall immediately on arrival.

A DERBYSHIRE STONE WOLF HEAD FROM ABOUT 300 BC LOOKS OUT OVER LITTLE WOOLDEN HALL.

hollins green and warburton

From the Black Sheep Craft Centre at Mount Pleasant Farm continue down Glazebrook Lane to the double lights and T-junction with the A57 and turn right on to the A57 Manchester Road, back towards Warrington. This dual carriageway by-passes the medieval settlement of Hollins Green or 'Hollinfare' on the right, which takes its name from the Old English 'HOLEGN' meaning 'holly' and 'FOER' meaning 'ford' - but this area is too recent to qualify for the Celtic period of this book.

There used to be a ferry crossing over the Mersey here first recorded in a murder trial of 1352 AD, but this was closed down in favour of the existing toll bridge some time after 1863. The stone jetty, bank defences and wooden piers can still just be seen on the Warburton river bank of what is now the Manchester Ship Canal. In 1773 it was recorded in the writings of a Mr.Thomas Pennant that the Mersey could also be ridden across on horseback at this point, "a horse passage into the County of Lancaster", which may help to explain further why the Saxons built their fort on the opposite Warburton bank close to here.

A short distance will bring you to a set of lights and a left hand turn towards Lymm and Warburton. Take this road. Although this is something of a detour from the circular route in this sector of Warrington it is well worth it as, like Winwick, Warburton has a fine network of suprises waiting for the traveller in history.

a viking comes home

The present name 'Warburton' may well be of Saxon origin as a fortification called 'WAERD BYRIG' is recorded as being built here in 915 AD and part of a Saxon cross was found in the bed of the Manchester Ship Canal, being removed to Eccles church for safe keeping at the time, but now sadly lost. This is interesting as the neighbouring site of Rixton, just downstream (MAP MARKED V), derives its name from the Scandinavian personal name for 'ERIC' meaning 'Eric's town' or 'Eric's place' following the Norse invasions of the same century. Does this mark some kind of military stand-off point from the 10th century Viking invasions of the Mersey Valley? The ancient record runs,

"This year (913 AD), by the permission of God, went Ethelfleda, Lady of Mercia,

with all the Mercians, to Tamworth - and in the next year (to) Eddisbury (914 AD)
- Then in the following year (915 AD), after midwinter, was built that at Chirbury,
and that at Warburton (WAERD BYRIG) and Runcorn."

At this time the Danes and Norsemen were attempting to invade from the West and often sailed up the Mersey on raids. In 911 AD the Danes had suffered a crushing defeat at Burnley and it appears that they very quickly left their military aspirations behind and 'Eric the Viking' simply settled in the area along with the various other cultures already present.

Ethelfleda's brother Edward then assumed the title of King of England about this time (the first time this title had been applied) and transactions from the period (eg. the Danegelt levied around 991 AD to provide a fund to buy off the Danish invaders) show considerable Danish activity at Warburton.

Warburton also lay on the banks of the river, the long-time border between the constantly warring southern kingdom of Mercia and the northern kingdom of Northumbria (the name 'Mersey' may be derived from the Old English 'MERC' or '(GE)MAERE' meaning 'boundary'), so a fort here provided a great defensive advantage to Mercia.

The 'BURTON' part of the name WARBURTON may be derived from 'farm near a fort' (TUN) or 'farm belonging to a town' (BURH) like the example in Sussex 'Burton' which was Budeca's (Bodecia's) farm.

Further evidence for the earlier Saxon pedigree of Warburton, however, lies in the dedication of the church to St.Werburgh who was daughter of King Wulfhere (657-674 AD) of the Mercians. She died somewhere between 700 and 707 AD and her Celtic emblem was the goose following the legend that she had persuaded a flock of destructive geese to leave her Abbey at Weedon by miraculous means and raised one of the flock back to life from a collection of remains after it had been eaten!

30 CM / 1 FT.

This leads to another possible origin for the village name, from 'ST. WERBURG'S TOWN' - 'WAREBURGTUNE' or 'WEBERGTUNE' as recorded in the Doomsday Survey of 1086 AD. A building known as 'Onion Farmhouse' located at Common Farm, Warburton, has a painting of an Elizabethan man and woman each next to a goose and a central Tudor Rose in a 'lozenge' (diamond) shaped surround, dating from about 1575 AD. It has been said that this may well be a representation of St.Werburgh and is the oldest surviving wall painting in the Trafford area.

WALKING THE ANCIENT LAND

Autumn leaves fell gracefully from September trees as a tractor turned over fertile soils now devoid of their bountiful harvests. The twisting river Bollin cascaded noisily past the derelict 14th Century Warburton Mill and onwards towards the junction with the Manchester Ship Canal where once the ancient course of the River Mersey meandered and could be crossed by ferry-boat in 1773 AD.

Here, in a field at the end of Wigsey Lane, next to the Abbey Croft land sold to the local priory around 1190 AD, three figures systematically walk the shallow furrows searching for evidence from the distant past. From the edge of the old course of the Mersey there comes a shout.

The group huddle together over a black basalt cobblestone about the size of three tennis balls and shaped like an egg. This is a two-handed hammer stone from the late Stone Age dating back to 5000 BC or more and is not the only find from this era to come to light in ancient Warburton.

TWO SIDES OF THE WARBURTON HAMMER STONE.

These fields and those next to the B5159 Townfield Lane have given up a fine collection of flints from the late Neolithic or early Bronze Ages. Five grey flints were found in a field next to Wigsey Lane in 1980 and a barrow-type crop mark has been noted south of Abbey Croft fields next to the Bollin (MAP NUMBER **9**) - with three more together on the west side of Townfield Lane, about halfway down the road towards the old mill (MAP NUMBERS **6**, **7** & **8**).

It is said that another barrow was excavated by Liverpool University in the 1950s near the course of the old Mersey, next to Warburton's high-level bridge over the Manchester Ship Canal (MAP NUMBER **4**). Sadly any records of this dig and associated finds appear to have vanished into the lost filing cabinets of post-war museums, unless no finds were located or the barrow turned out to be a natural feature and none were kept. A 1997 field survey following bulldozer clearance of the field revealed the extensive outline of the archaeological excavations but no trace of any barrow or finds remaining. Aerial photographs of the field are now the only evidence that a barrow ever existed here.

Opposite the old Hollins Green ford, on the opposite side of the first field on Warburton Park, a mound of unknown origin can clearly be seen jutting out from the rise at the far side of the field and another slightly elongated mound exists in the small wood to the right (MAP NUMBERS **11** & **12**). The visible mound at **11** may have been a defensive observation point for the ancient ford but the mound in the wood at **12** looks more like a small bell barrow from the late Bronze Age.

Aerial photography has also shown linear crop marks in the next field adjacent to these mounds, further indicating ancient farming or settlement in the area. According to Don Bayliss in his *Historical Atlas Of Trafford*, 'Beehive-shaped Querns' used by Celtic farmers to grind grain right up to the Roman period were found at Warburton in 1995.

QUERN STONE FOUND AT WOOLDEN HALL SITE IN 1987.   G.M.A.U. Archive.

Another burial mound exists at the centre of Warburton Park, north-east of the village (MAP NUMBER **5**), but this appears to be more recent than the strictly 'Celtic' period so we will deal with it in the later section entitled 'CONTINUING THE STORY OF THE AMAZING INVISIBLE VILLAGE'.

Coming over the Manchester Ship Canal high level bridge and through the toll gates you come to a cross roads in the truest sense, there being situated the old village cross steps, cross socket and stocks complete with a village well hidden in the private garden of the house behind. The cross is something of a mystery.

No ancient records of the cross itself exist except a picture of a similar cross in the village of East Hagbourne, Didcott, found in the church records and in the possession of the Warburton family. This picture shows a cross with a base between 1200-1300 AD, a cross shaft dating to about 1400 AD and a later Jacobean sundial and it probably represents a fair reconstruction of the Warburton cross.

Both the cross base and stocks first appear on the 1757 estate map, the stocks being repaired in 1764 and again around 1900. Prior to this one upright was in use as a gate post to a field and the other broken upright had been built into a cottage wall on The Green. The stocks must have been moved to their present site after 1890 as they are missing from a photo of the cross base taken in 1889.

WARBURTON CROSS 1889 AND TODAY.

At this cross roads turn right into Wigsey Lane (the ancient village 'high street') and park the car at the bottom of the lane to the left, in front of St. Werberg's church.

As you enter the churchyard through the typical Victorian Cheshire lych gate you are walking into the closing years of the 'Celtic' era. Possibly the oldest 'find' listed in this present book may well be the footprint of the dinosaur 'Labyrinthodon' that locals say exists in the sandstone side panels of this path into the cemetery enclosure, just beyond the church gate.

ST. WERBERG'S CHURCH IN THE 18TH CENTURY.

Mr & Mrs T. Lea

THE MISSING PRIORY OF THE KNIGHTS TEMPLAR

The fort that was built at WAERD BYRIG by Ethelfleda, Lady of Mercia, after the midwinter of 915 AD, has never been found, although it could have stood on the Warburton Park estate or where the church and Celtic cemetery enclosure are now, on the crest of a small hill on a bend in the old Mersey (still clearly visible as a long, low field feature at the back of the church today).

There is a 19th century Victorian record of a burnt wooden structure being found 8 feet (2.5m) below ground level when foundations for an extension to the rectory next to the church were being cut in 1837. In his 1970 book *Warburton, The Village And The Family*, Norman Warburton refers to a newspaper article published in 1955 which also states that the then occupants of the rectory had found the remains of charred beams and stone flooring the same distance under the garden close to the extension and the article attributed these to the Priory or one of its outbuildings.

Before rebuilding in 1645 (along with the church), the rectory was a thatched building said to have been the Priory dormitories or refectories and to be haunted by the ghost of a monk. The thatch was destroyed by fire in 1832. No more details are currently available and it is equally possible that the building found deep underground was the Celtic church, the remains of Ethelfleda's fort or the Priory site.

What has definitely been identified is the curvilinear D-shaped Celtic cemetery enclosure and outer-ditch surrounding St.Werberg's and in which the church currently stands. This is defined by a low bank about 3-7ft (1-2m) high which was excavated in the summer of 1997 and found to have a cobbled pavement on the crest which may represent the foundations of a very ancient wall or pavement.

A ditch once also ran round the outside of this enclosure but in 1832 the retaining wall at the front of the church was erected and the chestnut trees

planted. Up to this time the churchyard had sloped down to The Green and been surrounded by a hedge. Although 1996 and 1997 findings were, overall, inconclusive this type of banked enclosure is associated with sites in Wales, Ireland and the West Midlands dating to the 7th century or earlier (before 600-700 AD) and a yew tree growing on the bank was dated to the 1300-1400 AD period indicating the bank to be older than this time.

SAXON AND NORMAN KNIGHTS

By the end of the truly 'Celtic' era, Warburton or 'WAREBURGETUNE' was held by two Saxon freemen, Earnwig and Raven (who must have been Eric's neighbours). After the Norman invasion of 1066 AD these lands had passed into the hands of the invaders but not without resistance.

Local tradition states that the magnificent ancient yew tree just north of the church tower (to the right as you face the tower) was used to produce English bows with which to fight the Norman invasion. It was originally over eighteen feet round its base.indicating a great age for such a slow growing hardwood, which would also have taken many years to decay back to its present twisted wood core. The Rev. G.E.Warburton said the yew tree was virtually dead when he first saw it in 1872. It was dead except for a few branches growing on one side then it sprang to life again and the core of this tree still standing is believed to date back to the Norman period.

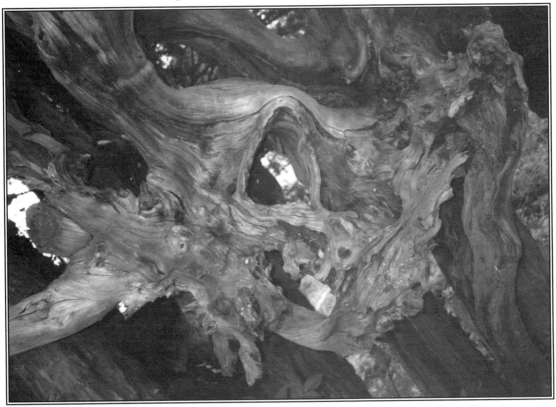

In his short history booklet of 1939 T. Newton states that the old tree remains once showed that it had been pollarded (cut back) about five feet (1.5 m) from the ground which is fairly firm evidence to suppose it had been used to supply bows in ancient times, possibly against the Normans, during the Crusades and/or during the battles of Crecy and Agincourt where local nobility supplied arms.

Sadly the English lost the fight against the Normans and, by the Doomsday Survey of 1086 AD, Earnwig's lands belonged to William Fitz Nigell, the Baron of Halton, and Raven's lands had gone to Osberne Fitz Tesson who also held the neighbouring areas around Lymm.

CISTERCIAN WHITE CANNONS

The order of Premonstratensian White Cannons was originally founded as 'The Brothers Of The Order Of Premontre' by St.Norbert at Premontre near Laon in France about the year 1120 AD. The first house in England was founded in 1143 AD in Lincolnshire with a number following over the next century, including Warburton.

In 1170 AD the two areas of land in Warburton were united under the ownership of one Adam de Dutton who retrieved the lands from the then Baron of Halton, Fitz Alured. Adam de Dutton's deed records that he obtained the consent of Agnes, his wife, to give to "God, St.Mary and St.Werburg" and "the Canons of the Premonstratensian Order (Cistercian White Cannons)" a "moiety of the vill of Warburton in free alms, for the health of the soul and Body of John, Constable of Chester (died 1190 AD) and his ancestors, for the health of the soul and body of Roger, Constable of Chester (died 1212 AD) and his wife." This document indicates that a church existed before the priory and that the dedication to St. Mary may be a Norman rededication over the earlier Saxon one of St. Werburg. Most Norman Premonstratensian priories were dedicated to 'Our Lady', ie St.Mary.

St.Werbergh's Priory is first specifically mentioned as existing in this deed of 1187 to 1190 AD, but the earliest charter held in St. Werbergh's Abbey in Chester includes Warburton and dates back earlier, to 1151-1152 AD, which would indicate that the first chapel was founded at the latest soon after the Norman invasion of 1066 AD.

KNIGHTS OF ST.JOHN OF JERUSALEM

When this deed was being enacted in 1187 AD it would appear that some land in Warburton was owned by the Knights of St.John of Jerusalem, also known as the 'Order of Knights Hospitaller'. This group of knights had originally been founded in 1092 AD as a non-military order to afford hospitality to pilgrims in the Holy Lands and to care for the medical needs of the Crusader knights, but they combined with the military Knights Templar between 1100 and 1150 AD in order to maintain a standing army for the defence of Jerusalem.

Adam de Dutton had two sons. The younger John de Dutton died in about 1190 AD and was buried at the Priory, but the elder Geoffrey de Dutton inherited the Warburton estates from his father Adam. Geoffrey joined his Overlord John Lacey, eigth Baron Of Halton, on the Third Crusade under King Richard The Lionheart and returned to Warburton in about 1228 AD knighted and with the Saracen's Head as his crest.

Geoffrey produced a son called Geoffrey who assumed control of Warburton in 1248 AD and the Priory in 1271 AD, followed in turn by his son Peter who first assumed the title 'de Warburton'. The next son, another Geoffrey, took control of the estates from Peter in 1314 AD and his grandson Geoffrey de Warburton served under the Black Prince in the French and Spanish campaigns of the period.

In 1402 AD Richard de Warburton became an archer for the crown and in the following year Peter de Warburton joined the Earl Of Northumberland's rebellion against the Crown. He was pardoned and later served under King Henry IV and King Edward V in France at the battle of Agincourt (1408 AD) as the King's "beloved Squire Sir Peter de Warburton". Peter's grandson Peter inherited the estates in 1448 AD and built a new family seat at Arley in 1469 although members of the Warburton family remained in the village up to the 1600'ds.

In Warburton the knights of St.John held lands right up to the 1600-1700 AD period and many traces of their continuous intervention in local affairs exist. They also became one of the continuations of the next order following the end of that order of knights in 1314 AD.

KNIGHTS OF THE TEMPLE OF SOLOMON

The Templars, or 'Poor Knights of The Temple of Solomon', were founded under Augustinian rule at Jerusalem in 1118 AD (or possibly earlier in 1114 AD) and had their Jerusalem headquarters in King Solomon's stables next to the site of Solomon's Temple on the Temple Mount, hence the name 'Templars'. They were most definitely a military order from the outset, sworn to the defence of pilgrims and the Christian faith but having also taken the monastic vows of poverty, chastity and obedience. They later became connected to the monastic order of the Cistercians with which they are now almost always associated in current literature but, unusually, they are almost always found at the sites of Augustinians in the Mersey Valley area.

Warburton is the exception to this being Cistercian in origin but may still represent the only site in Britain where the Knights Templar joined specifically with the Premonstratensian Order of White Canons. It is also thought from the name that the land round 'Wittenspithall' on the B5160 Duham Road to Dunham village from Warburton was owned or occupied by the Knights Templar prior to the year 1187 AD.

The Knights Templar and Knights of St.John were both known to hark back to the sites and traditions of the Celts, who still existed just a few centuries before them. For example, there is the well known Celtic 'cult of the head' which appears to indicate the Celtic belief that the soul resides in the head, hence the already noted legend surrounding the head of King Oswald set in a silver neilo shrine. It is believed that this Celtic tradition developed from the use of actual severed heads (800-100 BC) displayed round door ways and in oak groves, into the abundant stone Celtic head forms (200 BC - 600 AD+) found on buildings and sacred sites, and on into the Green Man or 'Foliate Heads' representing the continuation of the soul of the land's fertility (100 AD? - 1800 AD) and the previous Pagan imagery.

The Knights Templar were accused by the Pope of worshipping some kind of head when the order was officially dissolved in France by King Philippe IV in 1307 AD and again by Papal decree in 1312-1314 AD. However, some authorities think that this may have been the 'Turin Shroud' possibly owned by the order and displayed folded face outward.

Property belonging to the Knights Templar was often transferred to the Knights of St.John after 1314 AD for safe keeping and this may well have happened at Warburton. Many Templar knights relocated to Scotland at the time of Robert the Bruce after the order was dissolved, and it is interesting that there existed a fifteenth century Warburton, Nether Warburton and Airlie (Arley?) close together in the north highlands of Scotland near St.Cyrus (although any Templar connections here require further research beyond the bounds of this book).

Three Templar-type medieval stone coffins were found to the south-west of the church in the Abbey Croft in 1816 but where all the parts of these are today is not fully known.

THE WARBURTON 'GIANT COFFIN'.

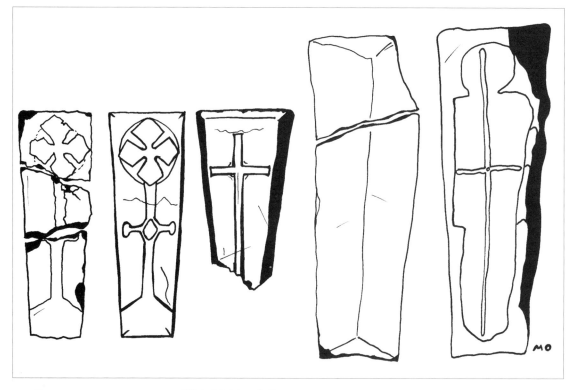

THE COFFIN LIDS OF WARBURTON.
FAR LEFT: AS SHOWN ON THE COVER OF G.M.A.U. WARBURTON ARCHAEOLOGY REPORT.
2ND LEFT: SAME LID FROM A 1970 PHOTO IN N.WARBURTON'S LOCAL HISTORY BOOK.
MIDDLE: THE OTHER LID ALSO SHOWN IN N.WARBURTON'S LOCAL HISTORY BOOK.
1ST RIGHT: FIELD SURVEY SKETCH OF THE GIANT COFFIN LID IN TWO PIECES.
FAR RIGHT: THE GIANT COFFIN BASED ON M.NEVELL'S ARCHAEOLOGY OF TRAFFORD 1997.

One coffin lid has been removed completely from the site and is illustrated on the cover of the University Of Manchester Archaeological Report for Warburton (SEE ILLUSTRATIONS). This has a variation of a cross of the Knights of St.John or possibly a Templar cross on the lid and probably dates from the beginning of the 13th century (1200-1270 AD). A second upper part of a lid with a simple straight line cross design is shown leaning against the inside wall of the church (next to the then-complete lid from the cover of the Archeological Report) in a photograph contained in Norman Warburton's 1970 book on the village and the family. This cross design possibly dates the lid as late as the 15th century.

The one stone coffin remaining on site resides on the right hand side inside the church by the wall, along with some masonry blocks possibly from a monastic building. This coffin is of 'giant' proportions for stone coffins of this period and type and, when it was found in 1816, it held a perfectly preserved skeleton over 6 feet (2m) in height. The lid, now broken in two, would take several adults to lift into place when it was still intact and the coffin used to be situated in the graveyard just to the south of the church after its discovery. It has no markings but is probably an early example, being part of the monastic foundation of the 12th century (1100-1200 AD). No trace of the skeleton remains.

The church now standing probably started life as a chapel of ease to Lymm parish but, from its foundation and involvement with the Knights of St.John in the twelfth century and despite a number of grants in the 1190s AD, mysteriously the priory did not prosper. In 1202 AD it became a dependancy of Cockersand Abbey in Lancashire and the Premonstratensian White Canons but Abbot Roger dissolved the priory one generation later in 1270 AD and sold it back to the local Lord Geoffrey de Dutton (Adam's son) at a time when both the Knights of St.John and the Knights Templar were at their height. Cockersand Abbey also ranked third in respect of revenue out of the religious houses of Lancashire and could certainly have supported any extra work undertaken at Warburton!

Geoffrey gave back the Canon's land south of the church now called Abbey Croft and asked for a chaplain to stay on to administrate his father's former property, pray for his father's soul and that of his deceased brother John whose body was buried at the Priory. This only lasted for another year until 1271 AD when even the chaplain gave up and sold the property back again to the heir, Geoffrey de Dutton II.

Although the parish church continued to use the land which it was allowed to retain, no solution to the mystery evacuation of the priory has yet been forthcoming and it simply disappeared from the pages of history! To add to the mystery, after more than ten years of concentrated archaeological exploration no concrete trace of the priory has yet been found!

THE SAND STONE BUILDING PHASE OF 1645 AD AT WARBURTON.

DECODING THE EXISTING JIGSAW OF THE CHURCH

The church has presently fallen into disuse and the key can be obtained from number 1 Beckett Drive, Warburton (the road diagonally opposite to the cross) or from the address usually displayed on the cemetery gate.

Once inside the church of St.Werbergh and St.Mary it quickly becomes apparent that the building is made up of a jigsaw of parts built round an early medieval oak timber frame. Dates going clockwise round the interior walls are as follows:

> The door through which you enter is in a wall dating back to the renovations of 1645 AD, like most of the neighbouring Rectory.

> The timber wall to the right with another low door in it dates back to the 1500s but the door may have been fitted from another building and has early English style capitals which may date back to the 1100 to 1200 AD period. It is thought that this door top was originally pointed not arched from examination of paintings made before restoration of the building began in earnest.

> The chancel and adjoining walls are also from the 1645 AD phase and it has been conjectured by archaeologists that there may be a secret, hidden burial vault of some kind immediately in front of the altar rail. There are certainly other burials under this church floor a little further out into the body of the church.

> The tower dates from 1711 and has an interesting hole in the outer front door which was used as a look-out for 'resurrectionists' or body snatchers leaving the churchyard by the gate on this, the only blind side of the church, during the 18th and 19th centuries. The former Sexton of the church, Isaiah Collins, who died in 1915 aged 85, could remember spending the night in the church with friends, watching the new graves in case body snatchers paid them a visit. Body snatchers also used a path down to the former river Mersey behind the old Pipe And Punchbowl pub.

Moving away from the walls, the oldest relics having clear dates remaining in the building are the bell at 1575 AD (decorated with the letters 'R.B.' and six fleur-de-lis) followed by the font inscribed "William Drinkwater the Keeper 1603". The Drinkwater family still live in the neighbouring village of Lymm.

In his 1939 booklet 'The Story Of Warburton And Its Old Church', T. Newton makes an interesting observation concerning internal alterations:

"Prior to these alterations (of 1813) the flagged floor was covered with rushes which were renewed each year at the Rushbearing Festival. The church accounts show that 10/- each year was paid for cutting and carting rushes to the church. After 1813 this custom was discontinued as the wooden floors to the pews rendered the covering of rushes unnecessary."

This is thought to be the oldest surviving photo of St. Werburg's church taken in 1889 and the photo below shows the same view taken in the January of 1998 109 years later.

The roof inside the church was once plastered and later painted in 1857 to represent the sky, sun, moon and stars along with painted or stencilled texts on the walls between the upright timbers in both church and chancel. At least two sets of texts were once written there, seperated by layers of whitewash, until repairs destroyed both sky and texts in 1867.

Further improvements in 1857 included the addition of the stained glass east window by 'Wailes of Newcastle'. This is a peculiar altar window as it depicts the resurrection instead of the usual crusifixion scene and has a medieval 'Templar' style red knight and yellow knight depicted lying stunned below the vision of the risen Christ.

WARBURTON OLD CHURCH NEAR LYMM.
C. 1900.

B.Griffiths

An old local legend once said that the wooden frame of the church was held together by deer horns used as pegs, but restoration to part of the roof sank the legend in 1927 when none were found. It was thought that the legend arose from the use of deer antler hat pegs fixed to several of the oak pillars which were later removed by souvenir hunters during the 1930s and 1940s.

Up to 1895 the main oak pillars were hidden behind plaster painted and shaped to imitate stone work. These oak timber supports are the oldest structural features being of medieval origin carbon dated to 1250-1395 AD, but this part of the structure on which the present church is centred may not have originally been used for religious purposes at all. Archaeologists have surmised that it was once an outbuilding to the priory, possibly starting life as the refectory or dining room. The presence of mouldings on the trusses are reminiscent of medieval banqueting halls and the uprights have been altered near the modern roof line indicating it was originally a much taller building. This supposition led archaeologists to commence excavations to the north of the church in 1997 in the hope that the wooden door in the earliest phase of the building had once faced the rest of the priory, possibly the cloisters.

Saxton's map of 1577 AD and Speed's map of 1610 AD also show the later developed settlement and deer park standing to the north and north-east of the church site, next to quite a large representation of the church.

Speed's map 1610

Work began on a plot of land at the back of a house to the north which used to be the 'Pipe And Punchbowl' pub in the 18th and early 19th centuries (first mentioned in 1746 and licence withdrawn about 1851). This tantalisingly brief one-day excavation brought to light the corner of another possible wooden building and a fragment of dressed stone at a depth of about 3-4 feet (1m) before a mix-up in land ownership resulted in the dig being closed down the same day. All was not in vain however, as one interesting story came from this encounter between archaeologists and local householders.

THE LAST TWO PICTURES REPRESENT THE ONLY PHOTOGRAPHIC EVIDENCE OF THE
FAILED DIG OF 1997. THE DEEP TRENCH ABOVE IS THE START OF A BUILDING.

FALLING INTO A MONASTIC UNDERCROFT

About the year 1967 two local men were taking a late evening walk with their small dog up the lane leading to the area of the dig when the animal disappeared down a hole under the last house. The men presumed that this badly blocked entrance must once have led into the old, disused cellars of the Pipe And Punchbowl pub, supposedly filled in by a Mrs Oakes many years before.

The dog was obviously unable to escape so the men cleared away the debris from the entrance and took their torches inside to retrieve the animal. This venture revealed a large and ancient vaulted cellar used for the storage of beer during the days of the pub, but of a far greater age than the building now above it, and answering the description of a medieval monastic undercroft. (A fine example of an undercroft exists locally at Norton Priory near Runcorn).

Should the story prove true, this cellar remains completely blocked up and in private ownership awaiting the future eyes of the historian who may step back into the lost Cistercian Priory of the Knights Templar!

THE FORMER 'PIPE AND PUNCHBOWL' PUB AND THE AREA OF THE FAILED 1997 DIG

CONTINUING THE STORY OF THE AMAZING INVISIBLE VILLAGE

Many important historic sites in Warburton are in private hands and not open to public view. These form a surprising collection of mysteries which could be termed 'the amazing invisible village'.

As has been mentioned, a strange burial mound exists next to the site of Park Farm on the Warburton Park Estate (to the east), traditionally thought to be the burial place of the Premonstratensian White Canons, Templars and Knights of St.John or the burial site of the Warburton family, whose ancestral home once existed at Park Farm before they moved to Arley Hall, Cheshire, some time at the end of the medieval period. This large square mound, over 57 feet (18m) in width and 9ft 6ins (3m) high, has never been archaeologically excavated and has a natural spring feeding a small rectangular pond on its north side. In the field to the east the ground has given way at the possible site of a well and many blocks of dressed sandstone masonry lie in the wooded pond site between the mound and the farm road to the north.

THE STRANGE BURIAL MOUND TO THE EAST OF PARK FARM.

All things considered, the evidence may support the existence of a small independent chapel or mausoleum constructed to serve the medieval burial site and neighbouring settlement of Park Farm.

This main farm, situated at the centre of Warburton Park Estate west of the monastic burial mound, has long been regarded as a moated site. Park Farm does possess a collection of very old brick and Elizabethan crook-timber buildings, its own chapel bell, a well, a very old pear tree and a square courtyard ground plan, but nothing has ever been found to support the legend that it once had a surrounding moat. The 'moat' feature in front of the main house may simply be an exercise in landscaping with a pond and stream included.

The only possibly 'Celtic' structure so far located on the Warburton estate may prove to be a large half-circle enclosure close to Park Farm observed during a field survey but which remains to be further investigated. Could this have been the fort built by Ethelfleda to defend the ford on the Mersey just to the north?

Apart from well marked and fenced public foot paths, Warburton Park is strictly private and not open to visitors without express permission from the Lythgoe family who have owned the estate for over thirty years.

A list of rentals in Warburton from Elizabethan times are now stored at the new home of the Warburton family, Arley Hall, and the earliest, dated from 1520 AD, lists 24 tenants on their Warburton estates under the unusual title of 'Inspeximus of the Charter of St.John of Jerusalem'. Did the knights and priory continue as a 'big church' like the one on Saxton's 1577 map, hidden to history for another 200 years or more and, if so, who produced the elegant and rare wall painting at Onion Farmhouse about 1575 AD? Who painted it, who is it and what it means only the Knights of St.John may ever know!

PARK FARM LOOKING UP FROM THE LEGENDARY 'MOAT' FEATURE.

Moving slightly closer to our time, it is worth noting the existence of more sites not visible to the public, which could otherwise be counted as part of the 'invisible village'. The example of the now vanished monastic cellar from the Pipe and Punchbowl public house is not an isolated one. When archaeologists undertook a recent survey of local houses they found that a curious transformation had taken place.

In the late nineteenth century almost the entire Warburton estate was revamped to a set style designed by the noted Victorian architect John Douglas. New buildings were errected including the new church of St.Werberg (incorporating the old font cover of 1595 and an ancient oak chest from the old church), the Church House next door, a post office and a school but far more significantly, the ancient village was completely clad under new bricks.

On the outside the medieval village has gone, but inside all the brick houses close to the old church of St.Werberg on Wigsey Lane and Church Green archaeologists found the original wooden houses dating back to the 18th and even 17th centuries, complete with inglenook fireplaces, wattle and daub walls and many other features. Like the ancient mysteries of the priory, these later relics of Warburton history still lie just skin deep below the surface waiting to be discovered - as one driver of a small earth moving digger recently discovered as it plummeted into a hidden well in the garden of one of the local houses.

As a parting shot it is said that the highwayman Dick Turpin was a regular at The Saracen's Head Inn on the A6144 Paddock Lane and used it as a sanctuary during the 18th century because; being in the ownership of the Priory of St.John of Jerusalem, it was out of the reach of the law at that time. Two other highwaymen were arrested at Warrington in 1769, and the treasury used to spend the considerable sum of £1500 a year to guard night mails on the principal local roads.

When The Saracen's Head pub was rebuilt by R.E.Egerton-Warburton last century, a secret room was found during alterations containing a collection of armour and weapons now stored at Arley Hall but, like the constantly shifting architectural sands of the 'invisible village', this room has also vanished yet again and the present owners have no idea where it is!

THE FRONT OF THE 'SARACEN'S HEAD' PUB SHOWING THE TWO ANCIENT STONE HEADS SET EITHER SIDE OF THE DOOR. THE CROWNED FACE IS A SARACEN'S HEAD, THE OTHER THE GREEN MAN.

RIXTON WITH GLAZEBROOK

ON THE ROAD FROM MANCHESTER

Drive back up Wigsey Lane to the cross and turn left, back over the toll bridge on the B5159. At the T-junction and lights turn right and drive about two miles down the A57 Manchester Road towards Warrington.

TO THE RIGHT

On the right hand side of the road lies a network of rich, peatland fields and the Rixton Clay Pits Nature Reserve, which have been studied by Lancaster University for their North West Wetlands Survey, the results of which have appeared in their publication *The Wetlands Of Cheshire - Book 4* of the series.

Extensive field walking produced a wide scatter of Stone Age and Bronze Age flint tools right across the Rixton-with-Glazebrook mosslands. These included 6 flints (4 burnt), 3 scrapers (one quite unusual and 'unclassified'), 6 unretouched flakes, 4 preparation flakes, 1 denticulate flake, 1 dressing chip and 1 unworked flint.A major gas pipeline was also laid across the mossland in 1982 and more field walking in advance of construction produced a scatter of about 10 more struck flints in this area.

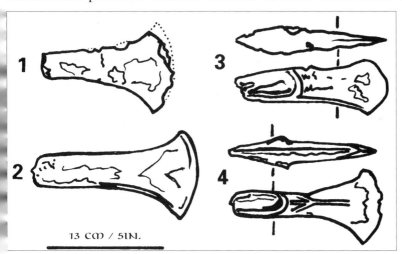

1 - A FLAT AXE FROM GRAPPENHALL.

2 - HAMMER FLANGED AXE FROM RIXTON.

3 - A PALSTAVE AXE FROM WINWICK.

4 - PALSTAVE AXE FROM LATCHFORD.

13 CM / 5IN.

Two Bronze Age axe heads have also been recovered here, one recorded by Dr.James Kendrick in 1861 and described as being "Ornamental with punched lines in a very unusual manner", and the other recorded by the Cheshire Sites & Ancient Monuments Record is simply described as "with punched line decoration and hammered ornament on the side" with no other details available.

TO THE LEFT

On the left hand skyline you will see the imposing mound created by the Butchersfield land-fill site under the control of U.K. Waste Management Ltd., who are based in the adjacent Rixton Old Hall moated site.

On the 1805 to 1873 O.S. map a Bronze Age tumulus is marked at the present edge of this land-fill site, on the southern bank of the river Mersey. This is shown as MAP NUMBER **10**. No record of any excavation of this mound can currently be traced although it may well have been destroyed long ago by slag dumping from Lancashire Steel Corporation's Irlam works early this century or digging for motorway ballast in the 1960s.

A little-known connecting road between the Roman forts of Warrington (Veratinum) and Manchester (Mancunium) is said to have approximately followed the line of Church Street, Warrington, passing through Rixton and Hollins Green and on into Barton and Salford, Manchester, where traces of it have actually been found. This raises all kinds of new possibilities for future archaeological work and possible Roman finds in this area.

At the junction with the M6 Motorway the A57 Manchester Road reaches two traffic islands. Go straight across the first one and over the M6 then turn right at the next island on to the B5210 Woolston Grange Avenue for Padgate and Birchwood. Keep going straight across the next four traffic islands through the Woolston Industrial Estate which will bring you into the Birchwood area.

THE EASTERN HALF OF THE MERSEY VALLEY O.S. MAP PRODUCED FROM SURVEY MATERIAL BETWEEN 1805 AND 1873.

THE AREAS OF

BIRCHWOOD

RISLEY

FEARNHEAD

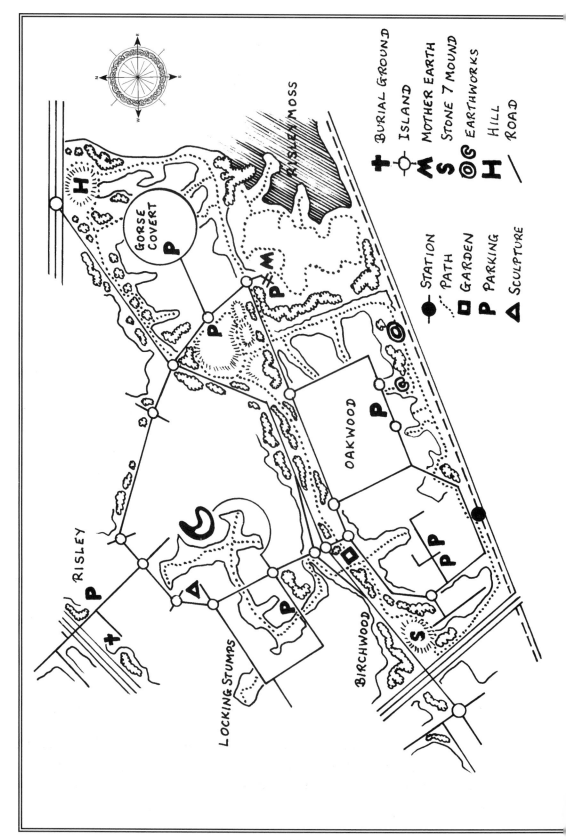

BIRCHWOOD, LOCKING STUMPS AND RISLEY

THE CELTIC ENIGMA

One of the real historical enigmas of the whole Celtic issue revolves around the supposed demise of the very culture that defined this creative race of people. At various times an invading overlay of another culture has temporarily masked the basic British Celt, only to be stripped of its best assets before the ancient Celtic culture rises again to swallow up its complacent conquerors.

In this region the basic Celtic culture began life as it did elsewhere, growing from stone through clay and bronze and into iron but with the unique advantage of direct links with all England by the ancient ridgeways, Wales by the Mersey estuary and ancient roads, Ireland by sea and Scotland by the later Roman roads north. Warrington became a major Celtic city-port and remained so for many centuries when Manchester was just a village and Liverpool did not exist.

Then came invaders to the region. Early tribes moving up Britain from the continent, ancient Britons, Romans, Angles, Saxons, Norsemen and Vikings, Danes and finally the Normans. All these visitors came to Warrington in war and yet settled in peace!

Did the Celtic culture simply collapse and die after King Harold's defeat against the Normans in 1066? Or, as these last major invaders joined the ranks of previously hostile war-mongers to settle into the peaceful Mersey Valley, did that ancient Celtic culture drift once again, like mist, from the oak groves and mossland islands where it had temporarily taken shelter?

The 'old religion' had still infiltrated the 'new' to become the chameleon of the church. Old sacred sites, ditches and mounds turned into churches, Celtic sculptures adorned the new buildings, Druidic ritual became medieval clergy, Barbarian Warriors became Knights with the Constantinian Cross as the emblem of the new 'Christian' church. Constantine was the son of the Briton Constantius who died at York in about 306 AD and, after the death of his father, he may well have set sail to make Christianity the state religion of the Roman Empire from the 'Estuary Belisama' of the Mersey and the Roman/Northumbrian port of Warrington - we will never know!

Taking over existing sanctuaries was also an officially approved policy of the church meaning that it willingly accepted the Celtic take-over bid. Gregory the Great spelt it out in 601 AD in a letter to the missionaries of the west:

"If these temples in Britain are well built, it is requisite that they be converted from the worship of devils to the service of the true God: that the nation, seeing their temples are not destroyed, may remove error from their hearts and knowing and adoring the true God may the more freely resort to places to which they have been accustomed."

This new state church appeared to have little thought for that small, peaceful band of twelve middle-eastern Jews and Gentiles who clung to their Messiah even unto death, over a thousand years before. If Joseph Of Arimathea did come to Glastonbury to plant a Celtic church when Jesus was still alive, a church that ultimately led to the conversion of the Roman Emperor Constantine 300 years later, then the new British church of the middle ages, a thousand years on, had seriously cut adrift of these early Celtic roots and the attitude of cooperation which first prevailed.

But a genuine belief never dies. Just as there has always been a small number of 'true believers' who still cling to the primitive, simple form of the Christian faith - so there remains amongst us a small remnant of the original British Celt not destroyed by the later church. This becomes apparent as you enter the modern district of Birchwood which has become a 'feast' of 20th century Celtic endeavour.

THE RESURRECTION OF MOUNDS AND MONOLITHS

The B5210 Woolston Grange Avenue is punctuated by four small traffic islands. Having gone straight on at all of them, the fifth and final island is very large and marks the start of Birchwood. Here turn right onto the A574 Birchwood Way which will carry you back over the motorway and onto the map for the Birchwood area. On the right hand side of this dual carriageway you will see the first of the new breed of Celtic site.

Here there is a conical mound topped by a circular bank inside which stands a large standing stone surrounded by two rings of trees. On the 1953 O.S. map this marks the spot of 'Lowes Farm' demolished to make way for the new carriageway, 'lowe' meaning a burial mound in ancient times. This new mound and stone marks the ultimate end of the Birchwood Boulevard industrial area and points down the boulevard and across the Mersey Valley towards Lymm on the opposite hills and the Midwinter sunrise.

At the end of the stretch of dual carriageway there is yet another small double traffic island. Here turn right and go straight on down a short dual carriageway to a big island by a petrol station. Turn left at this island onto Ordnance Avenue towards Risley Moss Nature Reserve and the Birchwood Forest Park. After going straight across another two islands either turn right into the Nature Reserve and park here or left onto Moss Gate, to the next island and left again into the Forest Park car park.

The New home for The Green Man (a short walk)

If you choose to park on the Risley Moss Nature Reserve you may have noticed that 'Mother Earth' sleeps on the left of the gate through which you enter. 'She' is an earth sculpture covered in grass and only the first of many signs that the Druidic 'Green Man' spirit is still alive in the leafy woods of Risley Moss.

It is significant that this piece of mossland now constitutes the only area of the ancient Celtic 'mossland crescent' open to public access between here and Lindow Common, the rest being in private hands, badly affected by development (as in the case of the Rixton Clay Pits nature reserve) or gone altogether. Here is a unique opportunity to catch the flavour of the Warrington Druid's world from 2000 years ago.

At this time in ancient history wooden 'causeways' made from woven branches and logs (like those found over the Somerset Levels, SEE ILLUSTRATIONS) would have networked the wettest parts of the mossland between the sandy ridges and islands of earth on which Druids and earlier shamans would have lived, worked and met to exchange notes, artifacts and magic crops like hemp, mistletoe, tree bark, herbs and potions.

THE 'SWEET TRACK', A NEOLITHIC PLATFORM ROAD THROUGH THE SOMERSET LEVELS.

The earliest finds on the mossland include a stone shafthole implement or 'stone doughnut' from prehistoric times dug up by a metal detector and taken to Liverpool Museum for identification in 1985 (the second one to turn up that year), an early corroded Bronze Age flat axe displayed by Dr.Kendrick in 1873 and a bronze 'awl' (a spike used as a hole-making device) which was found with other unspecified pre-Roman remains. These finds are hardly suprising in the light of the other Celtic evidence from this area presented under the section on Culcheth.

THE 'WALTON TRACK', ANOTHER EARLY PLATFORM ROAD IN SOMERSET DATED TO AROUND 2950 BC.

If you walk the fascinating path circuit of the Risley Nature Reserve and venture into the lair of the 'Green Man Of The Mosslands', you will eventually come to a large observation tower which looks out over the land to the distant hills beyond the Mersey Valley.

ABOVE: 'MOTHER EARTH' LIES SLEEPING INSIDE THE GATES OF RISLEY MOSS.
BELOW: A MODERN VERSION OF A PLATFORM ROAD SNAKES ACCROSS THE MARSH LAND
ON THE FOREST PARK WALK, BIRCHWOOD.

Climb to the top and gaze out over the mossland and you are looking at a collection of settlement features between Risley and Warburton that include seven circular crop marks, a D-shaped enclosure and evidence of ancient woodland clearance stretching out to Holcroft Moss and beyond. All these features were photographed from the air by the architects in charge of the M56-M62 Relief Road Link in 1993.

The creative work of the Green Man Spirit is often represented by sculpture displays along the paths over the mossland and photographic examples of work by Phil Bews, Lynn Kirkham, Richard Crank and Cate Clark produced for the 1997 'Artworks' project are shown here.

CELTIC CREATIVITY LIVES ON IN THE MOSSLANDS. CAN YOU FIND THE FACE OF THE
GREEN MAN CARVED ON THE SIDE OF THIS CRESTED NEWT?

The most important aspect of Warrington's Celtic past to be found here at the moss must be the mossland itself, and the chance to become part of the landscape once familiar to ancient settlers and Druids.

THE EARTH SPIRIT OF FOREST PARK (A LONG WALK)

If you drove up Moss Gate and turned left onto the car park for Birchwood Forest Park you are at the start of a large network of footpaths and recently created sites which emanate out from the Ranger Centre here as far as the M6 Motorway. At a slow pace it could take a full day to complete the entire path circuit shown on the map as a series of dotted lines.

Assuming that the route shown is used in an anti-clockwise direction starting at the east side of Gorse Covert, then the sites can be found in the following order: Pestfurlong Hill has been created almost next to junction 11 of the M62 Motorway, as a viewing point for the hills beyond Manchester and the Mersey Valley down as far as Warrington. The name originates from 'PESEFURLANIG' in use about 1246 AD and meaning 'the furlong where pease were grown'. This is probably in connection with a field belonging to the former site of Old Abbey farm on the opposite side of the M62 Motorway to the hill.

If the path is then taken along the A574 Birchwood Way back to the Ranger Centre, the Bronze 'Little Bo Peep' statue can currently be found staring out across the field looking for the rest of her sheep. Only one remains behind her.

Go round the playing fields and follow the path about a mile back down Ordnance Avenue towards Birchwood Centre, across a footbridge, and this will bring you to the Walled Garden which is a fascinating collection of plants and shrubs arranged with platforms in an oriental style, and situated inside a giant brick reserve water tank left over from the old ordnance factory that covered virtually all of Birchwood during the Second World War.

Following the path from here towards the M6 there are various minor mounds, stones and ponds before it passes the conical mound, stone and rings of trees at the top end of Birchwood Boulevard next to Birchwood Way. The path then follows the side of the M6 and the Manchester to Liverpool railway, past Birchwood station and on towards Risley Moss. On this stretch there are at least two circular earthworks to watch out for, one large and one small.

The path crosses Ordnance Avenue again and the mounds here at the side of the playing fields are empty bunkers formerly used for the storage of munitions from the factory. The path then returns to the car park. To the north, at the back of the Atomic Energy BNFL Pagoda building and the UK AEA site, a giant 'bean' shaped mound and 'contemplation garden' has recently been created outside the dining hall for the industrial estate, and a towering stretched-pyramid sculpture made from stainless steel mesh sited at the front of the BNFL building (marked on the map by a triangle).

This tour of Birchwood is but a brief taster of the new creative Celtic spirit that is rising once again in the last days of the 20th century.

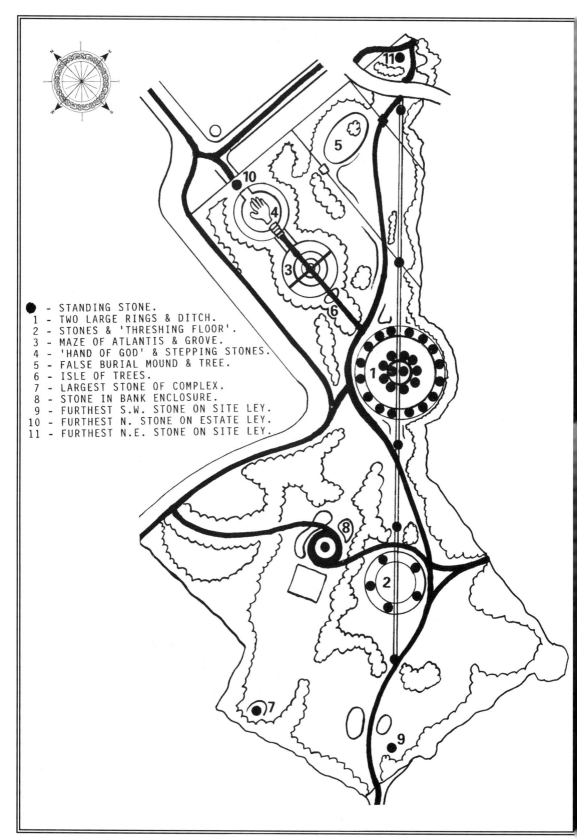

● - STANDING STONE.
1 - TWO LARGE RINGS & DITCH.
2 - STONES & 'THRESHING FLOOR'.
3 - MAZE OF ATLANTIS & GROVE.
4 - 'HAND OF GOD' & STEPPING STONES.
5 - FALSE BURIAL MOUND & TREE.
6 - ISLE OF TREES.
7 - LARGEST STONE OF COMPLEX.
8 - STONE IN BANK ENCLOSURE.
9 - FURTHEST S.W. STONE ON SITE LEY.
10 - FURTHEST N. STONE ON ESTATE LEY.
11 - FURTHEST N.E. STONE ON SITE LEY.

FEARNHEAD AND CINNAMON BROW

From either parking place, take Moss Gate up to the island on the A574 Birchwood Way and turn left. This will lead back to the dual carriageway and double island. Carry straight on until the large island on the far side of the M6 is reached and here turn right onto Crab Lane and immediately left into Fearnhead Lane.

Fearnhead and Cinnamon Brow are both in the area designated as 'Poulton With Fearnhead', names going back to the Old English 'POL' or 'PULL' meaning a 'pool or stream' and 'FEARN-HEAFOD' meaning 'fern-hill'. This area could justifiably be called 'The Fern Hill By The Stream' as Padgate stream passes through the area and the old hamlet of Fearnhead stood on a hill about 45 feet (14.2m) above sea level.

This first book on the Celtic aspects of Warrington would not be complete without the final site to visit, an appropriate place in which to rest the weary head having traversed the north-eastern sector of the town in a clockwise direction.

A FINAL RESTING PLACE FOR THE CELTIC SPIRIT

Having turned right off the big island onto Crab Lane then immediately left onto the old Fearnhead Lane, about a quarter of a mile along here on the right, before you reach the

shopping area, there is a pub presently called The Farmers Arms. Park on this car park and walk up the short Kings Road next to the pub (right turn off Fearnhead Lane) and, at the top, you will enter 'Parkfields' - which is probably Warrington's ultimate and yet best hidden modern Celtic experience (SEE MAP).

On entering this tiny park complex it will become apparent that there are a few small shaped mounds close to the path and a giant standing stone under the trees to the right. This is the first 'marker stone' of a huge complex of stones, earth works, ditches and mazes. In the field on the left behind the bushes is another marker stone, the largest of the complex, which faces down this field to a small half-moon shaped earth mound enclosure and another smaller stone.

THE LEFT HAND MARKER STONE OF THE COMPLEX AND POSSIBLY THE LARGEST.

Follow the main path from the Kings Road entrance and it will lead to a small circle of five large square stone blocks round a circular 'threshing floor' feature. Through the bushes and past a small marker stone further on you will arrive at a vast stone circle and ditched earth-works.

TWO VIEWS OF THE VAST STONE CIRCLE AND EARTHWORKS OF 'PARKFIELDS'.

This huge site is comprised of an outer circle of stones quarried in the Pennines, with three gates, an inner ditch, an inner ring and an 'altar' of two facing stone needles that have slanted holes cut in each. This sits on the central ley lines through the site and marked by red gravel paths. If the main ley line is followed it leads past another small marker stone to a false burial mound with a tree on top to the left, then on over a massive stone slab bridge, past another marker and across the road. Beyond the bushes and stream is the final giant marker stone at this end of the site.

Return to the huge stone ring and take the northern ley line and gate out of the circle and a short avenue of trees leads over a small mound and into a circular maze set out to the pattern of Plato's 'city of Atlantis' map surrounded by a wide, circular grove of trees.

Straight ahead is another grove of similar size with a 'hand of God' earth design marked out in sand-filled ridges and which can be reached over a shallow circular ditch on six large square stepping stones. Beyond this feature and over a small wooden bridge stands the last stone marker at this side of the site surrounded by bushes.

The road beyond this stone, which continues the ley line, leads to a housing estate on the right hand side which has two small stone rings and mounds of its own, then on into Cinnamon Brow park where the only genuine prehistoric find was made in 1901 in the form of a leaf-shaped flint, possibly an arrow head, before any of the present estate was built.

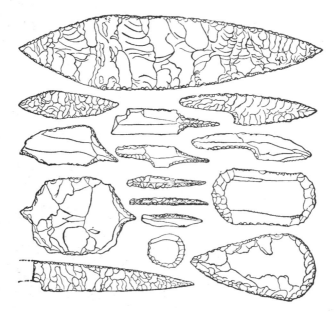

STONE AGE FLINTS OF THIS KIND HAVE COME TO LIGHT FROM FIELD WALKING ALL OVER THE NORTH EAST REGION OF WARRINGTON. TOP AND BOTTOM LEFT ARE FLINT DAGGERS. THE MIDDLE GROUP ARE FLINTS AND FLAKES. BOTTOM RIGHT IS AN ARROW HEAD.

The other local park at Peel Hall to the north-west also has a large 'heart shaped' mound and surrounding ditch complex with an ancient oak grove in the nearby local woods - but nothing to compare with the 'Parkfields' site, a magnificent work of the modern Celtic spirit.

ABOVE: THE 'HAND OF GOD' EARTHWORK STRETCHES NORTH FROM 'PARKFIELDS'.
BELOW: THIS PUSHPLOW, BARROW AND BASKET USED ON THE MOSSLANDS IN 1890 HAS
CHANGED LITTLE SINCE IRON AGE TIMES.

Here our first tour of 'Celtic Warrington And Other Mysteries' ends. As you sit amongst the standing stones or down a well-earned pint in the Farmers Arms contemplate this: are we not all just Celtic Britons at heart, searching for the spirit of The One that made us, the ultimate Mystery? - But that's another story!

TheEnd

THIS 'BEER LICENCE' WAS ISSUED TO THE LICENSE OF THE FARMER'S ARMS BEERHOUSE,
THOMAS BENTLEY, ON THE 25TH OF AUGUST 1883.

TIME CHART OF SIGNIFICANT DATES

Concerning dates, it is well to understand that the earlier dates are, the less precise their accuracy. Dates before 2000 BC can only be rough indications at best and are constantly being revised in the light of new archaeological discoveries.

The latest major example discovery is the copper mine under excavation on the Great Orme at Llandudno, Wales, which has proven that the mining of malachite copper ore was under way in this country as long ago as 4500 BC, almost 2000 years before some previously accepted dates for the Bronze Age. Further evidence of this came with the bronze axe head found with 'Otzi' the frozen glacia man of the Austrian Alps who dates back beyond 3300 BC.

Exact historical dating begins in this country with Caesar's expeditions and the Roman conquests of the 1st century AD.

DATES BC

OLD STONE AGE

35000	Paleolithic period: First bone & stone tools. Nomadic hunters in the Warrington & Mersey Valley area.
30000	Aurignacian period: First engraved & painted figures.
25000	Gravetian period: Paintings, shelters, 'Venus' figures.
15000	Magdalenian periods: Catapults, painted sanctuaries.

MIDDLE STONE AGE

10000	Mesolithic period: Geometric decorations, engraving.

NEW STONE AGE

5000	Neolithic period: Giant stone monuments, rings & burials.
4800	Probable period of first stones erected on Winwick mound & first known settlements in the Mersey Valley.

BRONZE AGE (EARLY CELTIC PERIOD)

4500	Copper mining on the Great Orme. (Revised Bronze Age?)
3100	First phase of Stonehenge commenced?
2300	First long barrows & main mound constructed at Winwick.
1900	Early Bronze Age: Beaker invasions. Stonehenge completed?
1500	Early Bronze Age: Wessex invasions.
1300	Middle Bronze Age: Rise of Urn people.
1250	Bell barrows & cremated Urn burials at Winwick & Warrington.
1216	Egyptian Pharaoh Sethos (Seti) II trades copper with Germany.
900	Late Bronze Age: Distinct Celtic culture begins.

IRON AGE (MIDDLE CELTIC PERIOD)

700	Halstatt period: Distinct Celts appear in Europe.
500	La Te'ne period: Distinct Celts appear in Britain.
450	Early Iron Age: Culture begins.
325	Pytheas the Greek visits, explores & maps Britain.
250	La Te'ne invasions of Britain.
100	Belgic invasions in Kent.

ROMANS IN BRITAIN (ROMANO-CELTIC PERIOD)

55-54	Julius Caesar's expeditions.
50	Belgic invasion of Commius.

DATES AD

10-40	Cunobelin becomes King at Colchester.
43	Roman conquest begins under Claudius.
43-50	Motte & Bailey defence structure constructed at Winwick?
47-51	Romans fight & defeat King Caractacus who is sent to Rome.
60-61	Queen Boudica's rebellion (Bodecia).
71-74	The Roman 20th Legion first recorded in Cheshire.
80-96	Roman development begins at Wilderspool, Warrington.
120	Roman 20th Legion constructs temple & station at Winwick?
122	Construction starts on Hadrian's wall.
140	Ptolemy records the Mersey as the 'Belisama'.
160	Roman Wilderspool at its peak of development.
175	Evidence for Christianity found in Manchester & Warrington.
251-356	The life of St. Anthony.
300	Picts invade Britain.
306	Constantine proclaimed emperor after father dies at York.
383	Last Roman soldiers withdrawn from Chester.

ANGLO-SAXONS (LATE CELTIC PERIOD)

380-400	Celtic city of CAER GWENTQUIC at Winwick about this time.
389-461	The life of St. Patrick.
425-459	Vortigern Chief of the British.
460-475	Ambrosius Chief of the British.
476	Saxon kingdoms emerge in the Lancashire/Cheshire area.
475-515	Arthur Chief of the British.
491-494	King Arthur in Wigan & Winwick?
516-520	Aurelianus Chief of the British?
515-540	Vortepor Chief of the British?
520-551	Maelgwn Chief of the British?
570-590	Urien Chief of the British
590-595	Owain Chief of the British.
596	Augustine arrives in Kent to evangelise(!) Britain.
560-600	Rydderch Chief of the British.
570-590	Angles begin to settle in Lancashire (eg. at Billinge).
400-600	Celts extensively settle in the Cheshire lowlands.
	Church first constructed at Warburton during this period?
593-617	Aethelfrith King of Northumbria.
605	King Oswald born.
613-616	Aethelfrith of Northumbria attacks Chester.
616-633	Eadwine rules Northumbria.
627	Eadwine and his Council convert to Christianity at York.
626-654	Penda rules Mercia.
633	Penda joins Caedwallon, King of Wales to attack Eadwine, who dies in battle
625-632	Paulinus visits Winwick & erects the first cross?
633	Caedwallon, King of Wales rules Northumbria.
633-642	Oswald defeats Caedwallon, rules Northumbria & dies in battle.
642	Penda kills Oswald at Winwick.
642-648	Oswin rules Northumbria (names are confused here)?
648-670	Oswiu rules Northumbria (names are confused here)?
653	Peada (Penda's son) marries a daughter of Oswiu.
	Alefrid (Oswiu's son) marries Cyneburga, daughter of Penda.
654-657	Peada rules Mercia.
654	Oswiu kills Penda and rules Mercia.
657-674	Wulfhere rules Mercia.
670-685	Egfrid rules Northumbria
674-704	Ethelred rules Mercia.
685-705	Aldfrith rules Northumbria.
689	Ethelred of Mercia (Penda's son) founds St. John's, Chester.
705-716	Osred rules Northumbria.

716-718	Coenred rules Northumbria.
716-757	Aethelbald rules Mercia.
718-729	Osric rules Northumbria.
729-737	Ceowulf rules Northumbria.
737-758	Eadberht rules Northumbria.
740	Aethelbald & Archbishop Cuthbert hold synod at Culcheth.
757-796	Offa rules Mercia.
759-765	Aethelwald rules Northumbria.
765-774	Alhred rules Northumbria.
774-796	Aethelred (I) & Aelfwald (778-789) rule Northumbria.
785-///	Egferth consecrated King of Mercia after Offa at Culcheth.
785-787	The Pope's synods at Culcheth.
///-///	Cenwulf rules Mercia.
789-816	Various administrative synods take place at Culcheth.
793-797	Vikings begin attacking the islands around Britain.
796-809	Eardwulf rules Northumbria.
801	Eardwulf attacks Cenwulf of Mercia.
801-805	Iona sacked by Vikings and 68 monks killed.
802-839	Egbert rules the English. 1st to be called 'King Of England'.
806-826	Vikings invade Ireland and begin to settle there.
809-840	Eanred rules Northumbria.
840-849	Aethelred (II) rules Northumbria.
844	Redwulf briefly rules Mercia & Northumbria.
839-856	Ethelwulf rules the English.
848-867	Osberht rules Northumbria.
852-874	Burghred rules Mercia.
855	Vikings attack the Isle of Anglesey.
856-860	Ethelbald rules the English.
860-866	Ethelbert rules the English.
866-871	St. Ethelred rules the English.
871-901	King Alfred 'The Great' rules England.
901-924	Edward 'The Elder' rules England.

DANES AND NORSE IN BRITAIN

902-910	Ingimund the Norseman and the Danes attack Chester.
911	Danes defeated at Burnley.
911-940	Eric the Dane settles at Rixton near Warburton?
915	Ethelfleda of Mercia builds the fort at Warburton.
924-940	Athelstan rules the English.
937	Ingimund the Norseman invades with the Danes.
940-946	Edmund 'The Elder' rules the English.
946-955	Edred rules the English.

955-959	Edwy 'The Fair' rules the English.
959-975	Eadgar 'The Peaceful' rules Mercia and the English.
975-978	Edward 'The Martyr' rules the English.
978-1016	Ethelred (II) 'The Unready' rules Mercia and the English.
1016-1035	Canute 'The Great' rules Mercia and the English.
1037-1040	Harold 'Harefoot' rules the English.
1040-1042	Hardicanute rules Mercia and the English.
1042-1066	St. Edward 'The Confessor' rules England.
1066	Harold II rules England.

NORMAN INVASION OF BRITAIN

1066-1087	William 'The Conqueror', the Norman, invades and rules England.
1070-1071	Norman earldom of Cheshire created.
1086	Domesday book records details of the Mersey Valley area.
1092	Knights of St. John of Jerusalem founded.
~~1087-1100~~	~~William (II) Rufus rules England.~~
1100-1135	Henry (I) Beauclerc rules England.
1114-1118	Knights Templar founded.
1120	Premonstratensian White Canons founded.
1135-1154	Stephen rules England.
1154-1189	Henry (II) Fitzempress rules England.
1151-1190	Priory founded at Warburton in this period?
1189-1199	Richard 'The Lion Heart' rules England.
1199-1216	John Lackland rules England.
1216-1272	Henry (III) rules England.
1270-1271	Priory dissolved at Warburton.
1272-1307	Edward (I) Longshanks rules England.
1307-1314	Knights Templar officially dissolved.
1300-1400	Distinct 'Celts' fade from the pages of English history.
1300-1450	Welsh Celts taken over by English Edwardian Kings.
1450-1600	Irish & Scots Celts subdued by English Tudor Kings & Queens.
1603-1609	James I, King of England, passes laws against Scots Highlanders' culture & language. The last Celts fade away?

APPENDIX

A small selection of books and publications used for this book, which will give the student a good standing on the subject of Celts.

NATIONAL INFORMATION

Automobile Association, *Treasures Of Britain & Ireland*, Drive Publications.

M.H.Bloxam, *A Glimpse At The Monumental Architecture & Sculpture Of Great Britain*, W. Pickering.

G.J.Copley, *Names & Places.*, Pheonix House.

T.Darvill, *A Glove Box Guide To Ancient Britain*, A. A. Publishing.

C.Dickens, *A Child's History of England*, Chapman & Hall.

C.&J.Hawkes, *Prehistoric Britain*. Pelican Books.

G.S.Hawkins, *Beyond Stonehenge*, The Anchor Press.

C.R.John, *The Penguin Dictionary of Saints*. Penguin Reference.

L.Laing, *The Archaeology of Late Celtic Britain & Ireland (400 AD - 1200 AD)*, Book Club Associates.

C.&J.Matthews, *The Encyclopedia of Celtic Wisdom*. Element.

A.Meehan, *Celtic Design & Illumination*, Thames & Hudson.

Ordnance Survey, *Britain In The Dark Ages*, (Map). Crown Copyright.

Ordnance Survey, *Pathfinder O.S. Maps For The Mersey Valley* (722,723,739,740), Crown Copyright.

R.Place, *Down To Earth - A Practical Guide To Archaeology*, Rockliff Publishing.

T.G.E.Powell, *The Celts*. Thames & Hudson.

T.W.Rolleston, *Myths & Legends, Celtic*. Senate.

A.Ross, *Pagan Celtic Britain*. Constable.

A.Ross & D.Robins, *The Life & Death of A Druid Prince*, Rider.

Earl Roundell, *Ancient Facts & Fictions Concerning Churches & Tithes*. Macmillan.

S.Savill, *Pears Encyclopedia of Myths & Legends: Western & Northern Europe*. Book Club Associates.

J.Sharkey, *Celtic Mysteries, The Ancient Religion*, Thames & Hudson.

L.Spence, *The Mysteries of Britain*. Senate.

R.B.Stoker, *The Legacy of Arthur's Chester*, Cevenant Pub.Co.

C. Thomas, *Celtic Britain*. Thames & Hudson.

N.Thomas, *Guide To Prehistoric England*, Book Club Associates.

A.Watkins, *The Old Straight Track*. Abacu.

LOCAL INFORMATION

A-Z Street Map of Warrington. Geographer's A-Z Map Company Ltd.

J J.Bagley, *A History of Lancashire With Maps & Pictures*, Darwen Finlayson.

D.Bayliss, *Historical Atlas of Trafford*, John Roberts Publishing.

W.Beaumont, *Winwick: Its History & Antiquities*, Beaumont Press.

H.Boscow, *Warrington - A Heritage*, Beaumont Press.

G.A.Carter, *Warrington - 100 Years A Borough*, Garside & Jolley.

Cheshire County Council, *Discovering Cheshire Churches*, Heritage.

A.M.Crowe, *Warrington - Ancient & Modern*, Beaumont Press.

W.G.East, Ed., *Lancashire, Cheshire & The Isle of Man - Regions of the British Isles*,
Nelson.

H.Fishwick, *A History of Lancashire*, S. R. Publishers Ltd.

D.Sylvester & G.Nulty, S. Grealey, *The Archaeology Of Warrington's Past*,
Warrington New Town.

D.Kenyon & R.Neave, *Lindow Man - His Life & Times*, The Manchester Museum.

M.Nevell, *The Archaeology of Trafford*, Trafford Metropolitan Borough Council.

M.Nevell, *The Warburton Archaeological Survey 1987-1995*, (unpublished), University of
Manchester Archaeological Unit.

D.Pickford, *Myths & Legends of East Cheshire & The Moorlands*, Sigma Leisure.

R.Richards, *Old Cheshire Churches*, Morten.

T.Newton, *The Story Of Warburton And Its Old Church.*

T.Strickland, *The Romans At Wilderspool*, Greenalls Group plc.

Norman Warburton, *Warburton, The Village And The Family*, The Research
Publishing Co.

Cheshire Archaeological Bulletin, Issues 1-9, Cheshire County Council

The Greater Manchester Archaeological Journal 3, 1987-88, University of
Manchester Archaeological Unit.

Historical Atlas of Cheshire, Cheshire Community Council.

Journal of The Chester Archaeological Society, Volume 70, Gee & Son Publishers.

Transactions of the Historic Society of Lancashire & Cheshire (Volumes 112-120),
Printed for the Society.

The Wetlands of Cheshire - North West Wetlands Survey, 4, Lancaster Imprints 5.

THIS MYSTERIOUS PHOTO OF A MAGNIFICENT CELTIC DOOR WAS TAKEN BY
MRS. WINIFRED MADELEY IN THE 1920'S BUT WHERE IS IT? AS SHE ONLY WORKED IN THE
MERSEY VALLEY AND NORTH CHESHIRE AREAS IT MAY ONCE HAVE BEEN A LOCAL LAND
MARK. IF ANYONE CAN IDENTIFY THIS DOOR AND ITS WHEREABOUTS I WOULD BE
EXTREMELY GLAD TO HEAR FROM THEM THROUGH THE CONTACT ADDRESS GIVEN ON
THE LAST PAGE OF THIS BOOK.